THE
ROYAL
PARKS

A WALK FOR
DIANA

The Diana, Princess of Wales Memorial Walk

BY TOM CORBY MVO
AND LUCY TRENCH

Picture Credits

The Royal Collection © HM Queen Elizabeth II

The National Portrait Gallery, London

City of Westminster Archives

The Royal Borough of Kensington and Chelsea

The Collection at Althorp

English Heritage

Historic Royal Palaces

Chatsworth Photo Library

Spencer House

Martin Jones

Tim Graham Picture Library

Cover photograph of Diana, Princess of Wales © Tim Graham

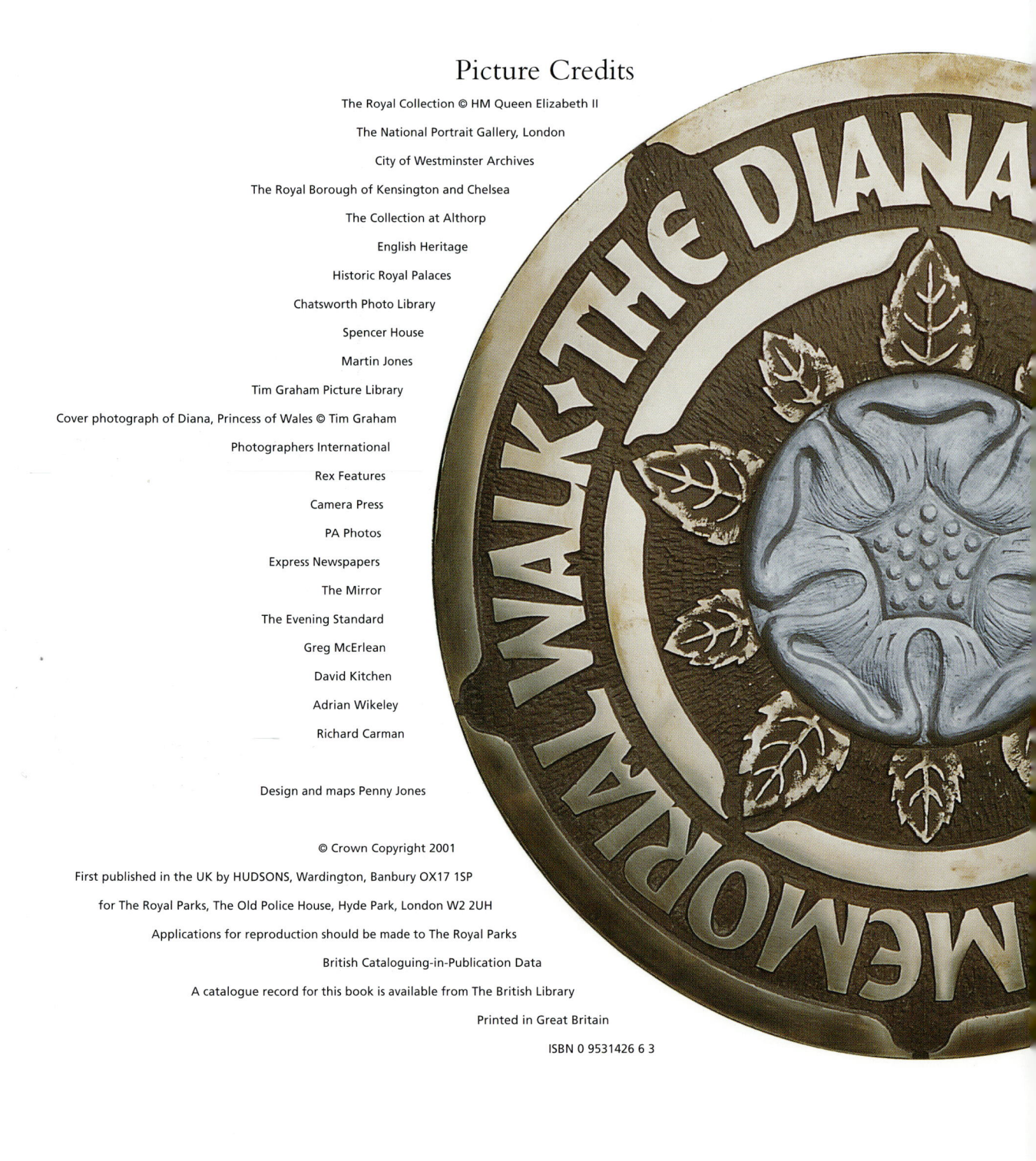

Photographers International

Rex Features

Camera Press

PA Photos

Express Newspapers

The Mirror

The Evening Standard

Greg McErlean

David Kitchen

Adrian Wikeley

Richard Carman

Design and maps Penny Jones

© Crown Copyright 2001

First published in the UK by HUDSONS, Wardington, Banbury OX17 1SP

for The Royal Parks, The Old Police House, Hyde Park, London W2 2UH

Applications for reproduction should be made to The Royal Parks

British Cataloguing-in-Publication Data

A catalogue record for this book is available from The British Library

Printed in Great Britain

ISBN 0 9531426 6 3

Contents

Diana, Princess of Wales *page 6*

Spencer House *page 16*

Buckingham Palace *page 18*

Clarence House *page 24*

Kensington Palace *page 26*

St James's Palace *page 34*

The Memorial Walk *page 38*

Hyde Park *page 40*

Kensington Gardens *page 52*

Green Park and St James's Park *page 66*

A Walk for Diana

THE Diana, Princess of Wales Memorial Walk takes visitors through four of the most beautiful parks in the world, and within sight of famous buildings and locations associated with the Princess during her life.

The seven-mile-long walk, which crosses St James's Park, Green Park, Hyde Park and Kensington Gardens, is charted by 90 plaques set in the ground, and along the way the Royal Parks Agency has improved and enhanced the existing environment including landscaping, restoring ornamental gates, fountains and memorials.

Chancellor Gordon Brown, Chairman of the Diana, Princess of Wales Memorial Committee, describes it as 'one of the most magnificent urban parkland walks in the world.'

From the walk visitors can see three palaces and two mansions which figured in the life of the Princess: Kensington Palace, Buckingham Palace, Clarence House, St James's Palace, and Spencer House, the one time town house of the Spencer family.

The plaques, the work of sculptor Alec Peever, have at their centre a rose emblem, etched in aluminium, which appears like a precious metal. The rose is heraldic in design, and while symbolising the Princess's enduring image, also symbolises Britain's traditions and heritage. The plaques are immediately recognisable at any point, and clearly direct walkers along the route.

The walk is one of two memorial projects officially opened on 30 June 2000, the day before the Princess's 39th anniversary. The other is the redesigned children's playground in Kensington Gardens. Together they celebrate the Princess's affection for the open spaces around her home in Kensington Palace, and her love of children.

Diana, Princess of Wales

The Royal Parks always had an allure for Diana, Princess of Wales, and so it is entirely appropriate that the walkway to commemorate her brief life should be routed through four of them.

The walk takes visitors close to places and locations strongly associated with the Princess. It passes the gates of Kensington Palace, where for 15 years she lived in the merged apartments 8 and 9, now sadly empty. She would jog and occasionally roller-blade in Kensington Gardens, and sometimes she would sit beneath a tree, reading a book and watching the world go by. Her sons, when they were small boys, would be taken to play on the swings in the children's playground there, close to the Elfin Oak, the tree decorated with fairy figures, the restoration of which Prince Charles and Spike Milligan took a keen interest in. The new playground, opened on 30 June 2000 and dedicated to the memory of the Princess, is a magical place.

And, of course, Kensington Palace was the main focus for the outpouring of public grief following Diana's death on 31 August 1997. The torrent of tribute, the flowers lapping against the railings, the messages pinned to trees, all spelt out a regard beyond her royalty. One note reportedly pinned to a bunch of flowers said it all: 'Born a lady, became a princess, died a saint.' Diana would have scoffed at the hyperbole, but that was what thousands believed. Diana was no saint, and was as full of human frailty as the rest of us. In life she transcended the division between royalty and celebrity; in death she became the 'People's Princess', and she probably would not have disagreed too much with that.

Flowers are still being left at the gates of Kensington Palace, particularly on anniversaries. Royal Parks staff periodically gather them up, and those worth saving are taken to local hospitals, including St Mary's, Paddington, where Prince William and Prince Harry were born. That surely is what Diana would have wanted.

Kensington Palace, September 1997.

The walk also gives a view of Spencer House, once the town mansion of the Spencer family, on the edge of Green Park, built by Diana's ancestor the first Earl Spencer in 1756; then, across the park, Buckingham Palace can be seen. It was from there, on 24 February 1981, that the engagement of the Prince of Wales and the then Lady Diana Spencer was announced. While the couple posed for pictures in the palace garden the Queen was holding an investiture in the ballroom. As the last notes of the National Anthem faded away at the start of the ceremony, the Lord Chamberlain moved centre stage and said that the Queen had commanded him to make a special announcement. While Her Majesty smiled with scarcely concealed delight, Lord Maclean read: 'It is with great pleasure that The Queen and The Duke of Edinburgh announce the betrothal of their beloved son The Prince of Wales to Lady Diana Spencer, daughter of the Earl Spencer and the Honourable Mrs Shand-Kydd.'

September 1980: the 19-year-old Diana with friends at the Young England kindergarten in Pimlico. The children called her 'Miss Diana'. In years to come the shy, downcast look was to become very familiar.

Showing the flag. Diana engulfed in an outburst of youthful patriotism during an official visit to Cullompton, Devon, in September 1990.

Across St James's Park, at Church House, Westminster, the Archbishop of Canterbury interrupted the deliberations of the General Synod, the 'parliament' of the Church of England, to make a similar announcement. It was greeted with applause and an East Anglian bishop rose to express his pleasure that a 'Norfolk girl', born on the Queen's Sandringham estate, had won the heart of the Prince of Wales.

The announcement ended months of speculation, but what few realised was that the 19-year-old bride to be was completing a page in the history of the Spencer family, which 251 years earlier had been thwarted by political manoeuvrings in its attempt to marry the first Lady Diana Spencer to Frederick, Prince of Wales, heir of George II.

Frederick admired Diana because of her looks and wealth, but the Prime Minister, Sir Robert Walpole, intervened and for dynastic reasons Frederick was married off to a German princess, 17-year-old Augusta of Saxe-Coburg-Altenburg. Diana became the Duchess of Bedford, but succumbed rapidly to tuberculosis, aged 26. Frederick lived on until 1751, perhaps regretting what might have been. He never became King, predeceasing his father by nine years. His son succeeded as George III when he was only 22.

The 20th-century Lady Diana Spencer, who up to then had had little experience of the highly sophisticated world inhabited by her fiancé, spent the early months of her engagement at Buckingham Palace, and may well have been bewildered by the protocol and hierarchical structure of the court; this despite the best efforts of the Royal Family to make her feel at home. But this young kindergarten teacher was no 'Cinderella'. Diana came from a family of grandees, and her engagement was the apogee of more than 200 years of intimacy and service between the Royal Family and the Spencers, who trace their pedigree back to Saxon times.

The Spencer family fortune was founded on highly successful sheep farming in the late Middle Ages. The senior branch became the Dukes of Marlborough, while the junior branch became the Earls Spencer. The family lived in great style. In the 17th century the diarist John Evelyn recorded that the furnishings at Althorp, the Spencer mansion in Northamptonshire, were 'such as may become a great prince'. The close links between the Spencers and Britain's sovereigns began with the Duchess of Marlborough, wife of the great soldier John Churchill and confidante of Queen Anne, the last Stuart monarch. Their daughter Anne married a Spencer, and the young couple were the parents not only of the unfortunate first Diana (she who never fulfilled her royal destiny), but also of the third Duke of Marlborough, ancestor of Sir Winston Churchill.

The formidable Duchess's great-grandson was the first Earl Spencer. His daughter the beautiful Lady Georgiana Spencer was married at 17 to the Duke of Devonshire. She was a dazzler and became a leader of fashion in 18th-century London society. She regularly gambled at cards until dawn, and when she ran out of cash would recklessly stake her diamonds. The Prince of Wales of the time, the soon to become corpulent 'Prinny', adored her. Georgiana's sister Harriet became the Countess of Bessborough and the mother of Lady Caroline Lamb, notorious for her ill-starred love affair with Lord Byron. The impulsive and glamorous Caroline, who can also be described as a Spencer girl, shocked even the libertine society of Regency London by her wild pursuit of the romantic poet. Early in their stormy relationship she described him as 'mad, bad, and dangerous to know', but she collapsed on hearing of his death in Greece in 1824.

Yet the history of the Spencers is not all passion and colourful eccentricity, but rather one of solid service to Crown and country. It is an impressive list: two First Lords of the Admiralty, a Chancellor of the Exchequer, two Lord Chamberlains and a Lord Lieutenant of Ireland. The

The tail coat look. Royal Ascot, June 1988.

Zimbabwe, July 1993. Diana visits the Red Cross Child Feeding Centre, Nemazura.

Facing page: Diana arrives at the Elysée Palace in Paris for a banquet hosted by the President of France. It is November 1988. The five day visit to France, with Prince Charles, was both a diplomatic and fashion triumph, inspiring headlines like that in *France-Soir*: 'Charles and Di reign over Paris'.

eighth Earl Spencer, Diana's father, was George VI's equerry between 1950 and 1952 and equerry to the Queen for two years after the accession. The Spencers have a background that is as colourful, rich and varied as that of any of the great families who have made a contribution to our national life. They also have a habit of turning out remarkable women: some who lived life to the hilt in the fast lane, some beautiful, some political, others simply content to do good. Diana was in fine company.

Now back to our commemorative walk. Passing through St James's Park, it offers a view across The Mall to Clarence House, the Queen Mother's London home, where Diana spent her wedding eve in a room overlooking the park. Clarence House adjoins St James's Palace, where Diana and the Prince of Wales once shared an office, from where they ran their official lives, and where William and Harry now live with their father. The Palace also contains the Chapel Royal, where Diana's coffin rested before her funeral on 6 September 1997.

It was 16 years on from the day at the end of July 1981, just four weeks after her 20th birthday, when she had starred in a transformation scene enacted in St Paul's Cathedral watched by 750 million people gathered around television sets in more than 70 countries. The marriage of Lady Diana Spencer and the Prince of Wales was, in the words of the Archbishop of Canterbury, 'the stuff of which fairy tales are made'.

The well-chronicled reality was, of course, tragically different. When the newly minted Princess of Wales – and, to give her the subsidiary titles acquired on marriage, Duchess of Cornwall, Countess of Chester, Duchess of Rothesay, Countess of Carrick and Baroness Renfrew – emerged from the great doors of the cathedral, the cheering crowds were witnessing the birth of a phenomenon. Who could have imagined that the uncertain girl standing on the steps of St Paul's, acknowledging the applause, would within a very few years become the undisputed star in the royal firmament? (Though it must be pointed out that the opportunity to shine so brightly was only afforded through her membership of the world's most famous family.)

Seldom out of the newspapers, always in the news, Diana used her sudden celebrity to fight for the causes she believed in. In the early days, before she became an accomplished performer, she found the interest of millions overwhelming. Her first official visit was a gruelling three-day tour of Wales, with its Prince. She was hailed as the new 'conqueror' of the Welsh, and the visit provided an interesting study in the

Diana takes the floor with John Travolta, star of *Saturday Night Fever* and *Grease*, at a White House banquet and ball, in November 1985. Travolta was reported as saying that his royal twirl was 'absolutely magical'. Among the Princess's less exuberant partners that evening were President Reagan and Clint Eastwood.

emergence of what was to become her familiar style. It was reminiscent of a younger Queen Mother, an acknowledged mistress of the art of small talk, but more direct, less caressingly gracious.

The Welsh tour was a great success, and *The Observer* newspaper devoted some column inches the following Sunday to an analysis of why the Welsh, not known for their respect for the establishment, had 'fallen so abjectly and hopelessly in love with Princess Diana'. Its correspondent Tom Davies concluded after some research: 'The general agreement was that Princess Di never comes on "posh", or "above it". Her behaviour in fact all pointed to her being "one of us".' He added: 'But the real key to her success must be the way she can suddenly stop smiling in a crowd and look around, for no obvious reason, with the purest terror in her eyes, as if a man in a peaked cap had just called, saying he was going to turn off the electricity. Welsh women, in particular, love this air of vulnerability, and their dearest wish would be to take her home to administer many cups of tea, a mountain of well meaning advice, and an aspirin to put her right.'

This was definitely Diana's tour, and Charles could have been forgiven for feeling a little discomfited when the Welsh made it obvious that it was Diana they had turned out to see. He took it all in a resigned and good-humoured part. As the crowds, chanting 'We want Di,' left him with a supporting role in his own Principality, he would call out: 'Diana, love, over here,' admitting wryly to a spectator in St Davids: 'I'm just a collector of flowers these days,' and to onlookers at Llandeilo: 'I haven't got enough wives to go round.' Later, as Diana's self-confidence grew, they took on

A visit to the Western Isles in June 1985.

Diana regularly did the school run. Here she is with Prince William and Prince Harry at Wetherby School, Notting Hill. Both boys went on to Ludgrove Preparatory School, near Wokingham, Berkshire, and then to Eton.

separate programmes of official engagements. Nothing could be more frustrating to a Prince with a serious message to get across than to be confronted with batteries of photographers and reporters interested only in the nuances of Diana's latest outfit and hairstyle.

The cult of the Princess – 'Diana fever' as it was popularly dubbed – had arrived. Diana was a mirror image in which millions of 20-year-old girls saw their reflection. The Diana look could be seen on the streets of Tokyo, New York, or Sydney, in fact in any fashion-conscious city. Certainly Diana was no stereotype princess, and in the history of the monarchy there has been no other princess quite like her. However, neither had any of her predecessors lived the way she did. They may have faced war, plague or dynastic strife, but they did not have to survive permanently in a glaring spotlight, and Diana's two immediate predecessors, Alexandra of Denmark and Mary of Teck, had the advantage of a respectful, even obsequious, press.

Diana was labelled by the media in many ways, but the glib tags failed to reach the core of her many-faceted personality. Her first incarnation was as a sweet and unassuming kindergarten teacher, the 'Sloane Ranger' who in her unworldly way posed for a photograph wearing an almost see-through skirt with the sun behind her. From 'Shy Di', blushing demurely beneath her heavy fringe, she became 'Disco Di', or 'Dallasty Di'. Then the headline writers created 'Caring Di' and 'Crusading Di', prompted by her tackling of causes that others hesitated to take on: causes that were considered difficult, such as AIDS in the early days after its identification; unfashionable, such as leprosy; or politically controversial, such as the banning of landmines, her final crusade.

She was fully aware of her impact, and used her photogenic glamour to good effect. For instance, she knew that the photograph would go round the world if she made a point of shaking hands with the AIDS patients she met when she opened a special unit at the Middlesex Hospital. It was her determined effort to explode the myth that simple social contact can spread the disease. Fear of being identified was so strong among the victims she spoke to that day, that only one man among nine agreed to be photographed. Diana was saddened when he died two months later.

11

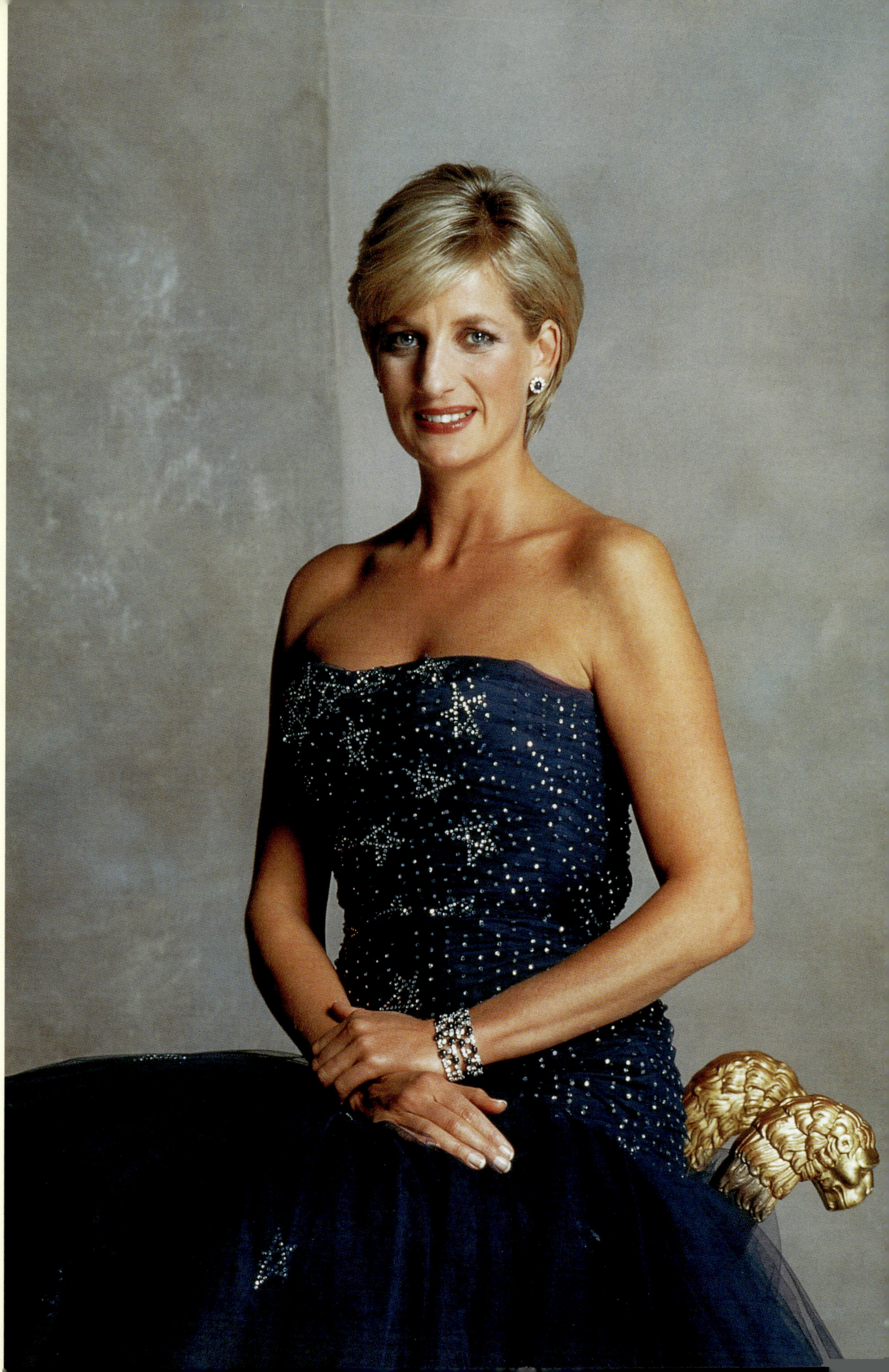

Arriving for a gala evening at the Serpentine Gallery, in Kensington Gardens, on 30 June 1994.

Rain soaked Latin gallantry. A kiss on the hand from Pavarotti when Diana and Prince Charles attended a charity concert in Hyde Park on 31 July 1991.

Facing page: a formal portrait from 1987.

Then there was her insistence on clasping the diseased hands of young sufferers of leprosy during a visit to Indonesia, dispelling some of the superstition that still surrounds what is regarded by the uninformed as a Biblical scourge. She showed considerable interest in the work of Relate, formerly the National Marriage Guidance Council, sitting in on therapy sessions and listening at a discreet distance while couples discussed their problems with a counsellor. She championed the mentally handicapped; attacked television 'soaps', despite being a fan of *Eastenders*, for encouraging people to drink; and warned how drink and drug addiction could wreck families. On a solo visit to New York she went downtown to a district infested with drug dealing, crime and violence, touching the heart of this toughest of cities when she picked up and hugged a seven-year-old boy dying of AIDS in the paediatric unit of Harlem Hospital. It was another symbolic act, and again the picture was published around the world.

As the years went by, Diana evolved as a determined, committed and skilful international figure, and her warmth and gift of communication did much to popularise the monarchy. But she never totally escaped from the media mythology that was always threatening to engulf her. One friend, herself a journalist, attempting to interpret some of the press coverage of the years in which Diana was Princess of Wales, declared: 'It was like reading about an alien, because the woman described simply did not exist.' Millions of women fantasised about changing places with her, but those who were favoured with her confidence knew that she sometimes longed for the ordinary humdrum routine of their lives. 'They don't know how lucky they are,' she once remarked. Diana knew the power of her glamour, but at the same time loathed the 'clothes horse' image that became so firmly attached to her in her early years as a royal, and which just would not go away. Several years before she died her staff stopped handing out the slips of paper to reporters describing what she was wearing for official engagements. It didn't work, because the media continued to take an obsessive interest in her as a fashion icon; and there was no doubt about it, she did love clothes.

In Washington, in October 1990, Diana makes a dream come true for a three-year-old girl seriously ill with Aids. The Princess met the little girl, identified only by her nick-name of 'First Lady' at a children's home. And when 'First Lady' asked: 'Can I ride in your car?' Diana swept her up in her arms and carried her into the back of her Rolls-Royce for a spin.

The last crusade. Diana in landmine infested Angola in January 1997.

After the collapse of her marriage was formalised the Princess gave up the patronage and presidencies of almost 100 charities, to concentrate on just six in which she was particularly interested: Centrepoint, the charity for the homeless; the National Aids Trust; the Leprosy Mission; the English National Ballet; the Great Ormond Street Hospital for Sick Children; and the Royal Marsden Hospital, which specialises in cancer treatment and research. Then, following her divorce in August 1996, she started to create a new life for herself and early in 1997 travelled to Angola to support the Red Cross campaign for a ban on landmines. The visit was a great success and focused world attention on the issue, attention Diana capitalised on with a trip to Bosnia. Two months before her death 79 of her dresses were auctioned by Christie's in New York, raising £3.5 million for cancer and AIDS charities. Each dress symbolised a phase in her life and a break from the past. The sale was the suggestion of Prince William, and some of the gowns went on display in Kensington Palace.

On 21 July Diana carried out her last official engagement, a visit to the children's unit at Northwick Park and St Mark's Hospital in north-west London. Five weeks later the news of her death, in Paris, reverberated around an unbelieving world. One can only speculate at what turns her life might have taken if she had survived, but surely her commitment to the destitute, the sick, the overlooked and the dispossessed would have continued. Above all she would have remained an adoring mother, adored by her sons. How proud now she would have been of the development of 'my boys', as she called them.

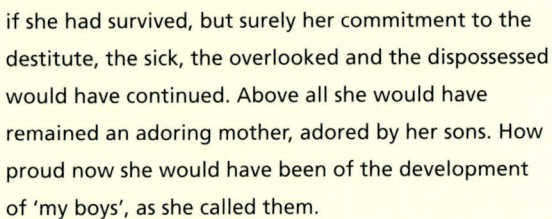

Unfortunately the myth is already overtaking the woman, forever young, and bracketed in the public consciousness with other icons cut down in comparative youth, such as Marilyn Monroe and James Dean. The comparisons are probably mistaken, and do her less than justice, although, like Monroe and Dean, Diana had star quality. The difference is that Diana will be remembered for the good she did and for the tragic waste of her potential to enhance the lives of others. While the memory of these 'megastars' will eventually find its rightful place, that of Diana will remain secure in the context of history.

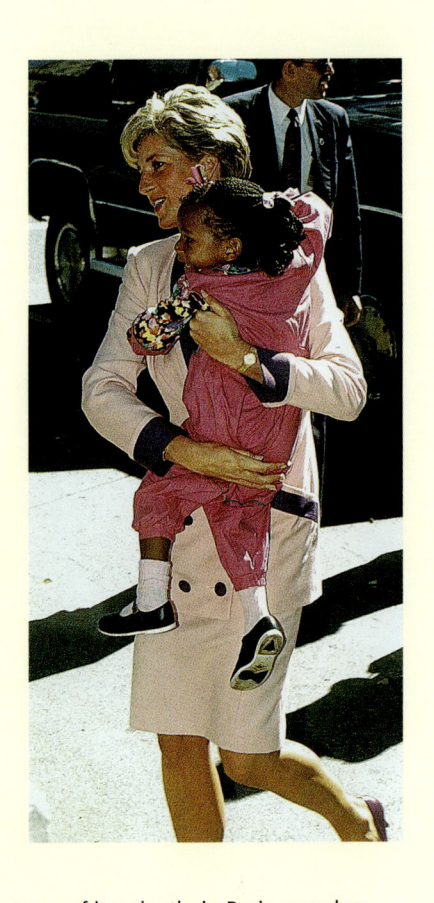

6 September 1997. The Princess's funeral cortège passes the Houses of Parliament.

Spencer House

Spencer House c1800.

Sarah Jennings, Duchess of Marlborough, Princess Diana's redoubtable ancestress.

The first Earl Spencer by Gainsborough.

Spencer House, once the town house of the Spencers of Althorp, has always been recognised as one of London's most magnificent private palaces. It was largely the ambitious creation of John, the first Earl Spencer, who began to build it in 1756 (to a design by John Vardy) as part of the network of splendid mansions constructed by a politically minded aristocracy.

These were houses built to impress, settings in which families such as the Spencers could enhance their prestige and influence. Geographically close, they frequently competed in brilliance with the official Court at St James's Palace and Buckingham House (later Buckingham Palace). Devonshire House, the mansion of the Duke of Devonshire (who in 1774 took as his wife Earl Spencer's ravishing daughter Georgiana, the original Spencer girl) also looked out over Green Park and from its windows could be seen Spencer House and Buckingham House. Devonshire House is long gone, but its gates, the Devonshire Gates, now form one of the entrances to the park.

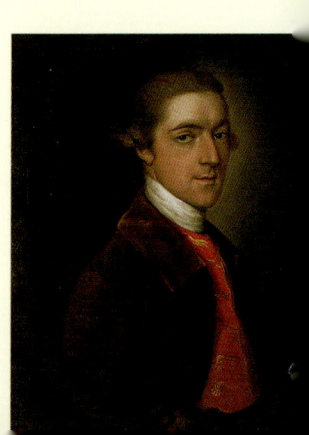

Spencer House, however, is London's only great 18th-century town house to survive intact, a fact that is a tribute to its successive custodians. Spencer House took ten years to complete, and cost almost £50,000. The first Earl could afford it, however, as he inherited, while still a minor, the fortunes of both the Duchess of Marlborough and of his grandfather the Earl of Sunderland. He was only 11 years old when his own father died, leaving an estate worth £750,000 (£45 million by today's arithmetic). Young John Spencer had £700 a week to spend, at a time when a gentleman could live comfortably on £300 a year. His inheritance included 100,000 acres, five houses and a collection of plate, diamonds and paintings. When in 1755 he married the 18-year-old Georgiana Poyntz, daughter of a member of George II's Privy Council, the diamond buckles on his honeymoon shoes alone were said to be worth £30,000.

The fabulously wealthy Spencers then set about building a grand new London home where, as members of the tight circle of Whig families at the very top of society, they could entertain, dispense patronage and influence affairs. The house, which also became a repository for Earl Spencer's collection of art and classical antiquities, was described in 1772 by the travel writer Arthur Young thus: 'I do not apprehend there is a house in England of its size better worth the view of the curious in architecture and the fitting up and furnishing of great houses than Lord Spencer's in St James's Place.'

The marriage between John Spencer and Georgiana Poyntz was a love match. In the Painted Room of their house the theme is the Triumph of Love and, more significantly, their own union. In an inset painted panel Hymen, the god of marriage, draws back the robes worn by Venus; a Venus whose features could be those of Georgiana, Countess Spencer.

Spencer House remained the home of the Spencer family until 1895, when it was let to a series of tenants, but the family returned following the death of the fifth Earl in 1910 and in 1926 the building was substantially restored and redecorated by the seventh Earl, Princess Diana's grandfather. It was largely due to his efforts that Spencer House did not suffer demolition, like so many other large London houses, in the period between the two World Wars. After the Spencers finally left, the house was occupied until 1943 by the Ladies' Army and Navy Club. It was damaged by a bomb blast in 1944 and after the war Christie's, the auctioneers, moved in, to be followed by other tenants until in 1985 the lease was acquired by RIT Capital Partners plc. Under the chairmanship of Lord Rothschild, Spencer House has been painstakingly restored to its original grandeur. Princess Diana once again kept a date with history when she performed the reopening ceremony in November 1990.

Eight rooms are open to the public for viewing on Sundays, and are also available for private and corporate entertaining during the rest of the week.

Countess Spencer and her daughter, Georgiana, later Duchess of Devonshire, by Sir Joshua Reynolds.

Georgiana, Duchess of Devonshire, by Reynolds.

The Palm Room, Spencer House.

17

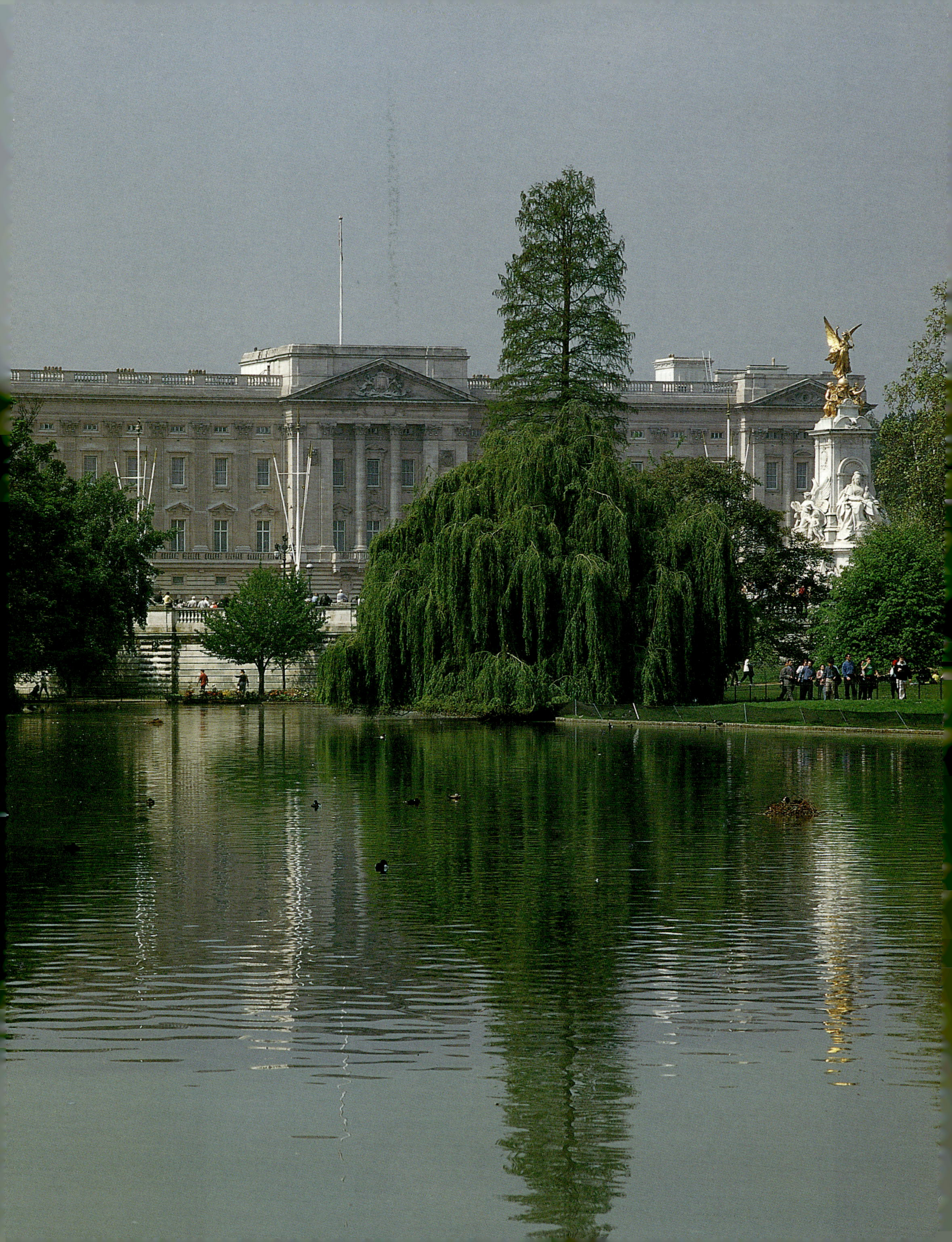

Buckingham Palace

Buckingham Palace is the headquarters of a working monarchy. Very often the last light to be turned off is that in the Queen's first-floor study, overlooking Constitution Hill, after a long evening spent sifting through the red boxes of state papers that follow her everywhere, even on holiday. On one such occasion, and it was a particularly heavy session with 'the boxes', the Queen is said to have remarked to the lady-in-waiting who had shared the night watch with her: 'You know, I do work awfully hard, but Mummy (a reference to Queen Elizabeth, the Queen Mother) has all the charm.'

Her Majesty was underestimating herself, because she is funny, wry and has a delightful sense of irony. She also has bags of common sense, and it was she who, in 1993, hit upon the idea of opening Buckingham Palace to the paying public, as a way of helping to meet the cost of restoring fire-ravaged Windsor Castle.

The great lyricist and friend of royalty Sir Noel Coward wrote wittily about the impoverished owners of 'The Stately Homes of England' having to dispose of 'rows and rows and rows of Gainsboroughs and Lawrences' to preserve their family seats for future generations. Her Majesty, of course, would never be so reduced, but the logic was inescapable.

An aerial view of Buckingham Palace. Behind the façade can be glimpsed Nash's elegant portico, which formed part of the original east front.

Facing page: the Palace viewed from the lake in St James's Park.

Why not let the glories of one palace pay for the restoration of another? It was a pragmatic way of dealing with an unexpected £40 million bill, and based on the belief that all those thousands of people who gathered, rain or shine, 365 days of the year, to peer through the splendidly ornate gilded gates and railings installed by command of George V were just itching to see inside. The Queen and her courtiers were right, and the palace has become one of the hottest tourist properties in town.

So what do the 400,000 or so paying visitors a year see? Certainly not 'rows and rows and rows of Gainsboroughs and Lawrences', nor, as Sir Noel's lyric continues, 'some sporting prints of Aunt Florence's, which are really rather rude', though there are some (not rude) cartoons in the loos. Neither do they get even the merest glimpse of the Queen's relatively simply furnished private apartments, where she has lived since she moved from Clarence House – her first home as a young married woman – after her accession to the throne on the premature death of her father, George VI, in 1952. Visitors see only the State Rooms, but an essential ingredient of their visit is its mystery, what they cannot see, and the strong feeling that they are, in fact, in somebody's home: a place where children have slid across polished floors; where a 19-year-old Princess in waiting practised ballet and tap routines to pass the time in the days leading to her July 1981 wedding; or where the Queen, said to be skilled at putting on a tiara while running down the stairs, might make a final adjustment in one of the long wall mirrors before making her entrance to greet guests at a State Banquet.

The senses are at once assailed by the grandeur of it all, maybe not so extravagant as Versailles, but still very remarkable indeed; by the deep pink, cream, blue, gold and white decoration, by the

Balcony scene. The Prince and Princess of Wales on the Palace balcony after their marriage at St Paul's Cathedral, on 29 July 1981.

crystal chandeliers, the exquisite workmanship of the furniture and porcelain – some of it the former property of dispossessed French aristocrats and bought by that most extravagant of collectors the Prince Regent, later George IV, in the aftermath of the French Revolution. But what tantalises many visitors is what lies behind the locked, highly polished wooden and gilt doors that lead to off-limits areas. The answer is: 52 royal and guest bedrooms, 188 staff bedrooms, 92 offices, 78 bathrooms and lavatories, a kitchen complex, staff dining rooms, a cinema, the court post office, a police station and a swimming pool once frequently used by Princess Diana and Princess Margaret.

Buckingham Palace is a very busy place, with constant comings and goings; incoming ambassadors to present their credentials, bishops to 'do homage' on appointment, judges, and hundreds of official callers whose business is concerned with that of the world's most famous monarchy. While Parliament is in session the Prime Minister arrives every Tuesday at 6.30 p.m. for his weekly audience with the Queen. Tony Blair is Her Majesty's tenth Prime Minister, and like his predecessors is listened to carefully and questioned adroitly by the woman who, because of the length of her reign and extent of her experience, is probably better informed on politics than any other in Britain. Then there are the 'getting to know you' receptions and lunches, two full-scale State Visits a year, and in summer three garden parties, attended by 27,000 guests.

All this, and the organisation and running of the Queen's official programme, let alone that of Prince Philip and other members of the Royal Family, means a lot of work. Almost 400 people are employed at Buckingham Palace, and if a visitor did manage to escape the vigilant eye of one of the attendants that discreetly patrol the State Rooms during the public opening and stray behind those imposing doors, he or she could face a roomful of surprised secretaries, busy behind their computers, or a footman cleaning silver.

The present palace is the culmination of several remodellings from previous houses. There was once a mulberry garden on the site, planted by James I to encourage the silk industry, but the royal gardeners were less than assiduous in their homework and planted black mulberries, rather than the white variety on which silkworms feed. The mulberry garden then degenerated into what amounted to an open-air brothel, which according to the diarist Samuel Pepys, was a draw for a 'rascally, whoring, roguing' class of person.

Buckingham House, bought by George III in 1762 as a family home. This picture dates from 1819 before George IV's rebuilding and the creation of Buckingham Palace.

George IV, as Prince Regent in 1814, by Sir Thomas Lawrence.

Diana meets World War II veterans outside Buckingham Palace during the celebration to mark the 50th anniversary of VJ Day.

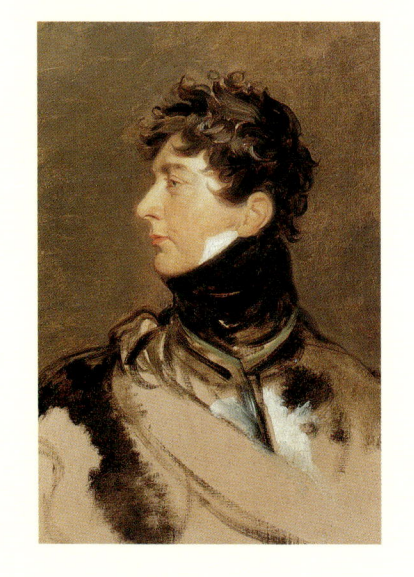

The first building on the site was built in 1677 for Lord Arlington. It was transformed and enlarged in 1702–5, when the first Duke of Buckingham and Normanby built himself a redbrick country house at the interface of the Charles II's new canal and Mall. The Duke was delighted with his new house and wrote, 'The avenues … are along St James's Park, through rows of goodly elms on one hand, and gay flourishing elms on the other.' Queen Anne, however, was not pleased, since it now appeared that the royal park was laid out for the house, rather than vice versa. The solution, which did not materialise until 1762, was for the monarch to buy Buckingham House. It was purchased by George III for £28,000 as a family home and known as the Queen's House. Fourteen of his children were born there.

The creation of Buckingham Palace as a symbol of national greatness, after the victories of the Napoleonic wars, was due to George IV, who, despite a dissolute private life, had the most exquisite taste when it came to buildings, pictures and furniture. He declared that Carlton House, on which he had spent a prodigious amount of money, was unsuitable for a King of England and that Buckingham House, his childhood home, must be rebuilt. The government reluctantly agreed that a sum that 'might not be less than £200,000' should be spent on its 'repair and improvement', while the King instructed John Nash to rebuild and enlarge the house in Bath stone. The bill eventually came to £700,000.

Buckingham Palace in 1846, before the removal of the Marble Arch.

Unfortunately, Nash's design is now largely invisible to the public. The east front, with its fine, two-storey portico, originally opened onto a deep forecourt (which can still be glimpsed through the present entrances) before which stood Marble Arch. The west front, which is unaltered, is a long, low composition in Bath stone with a bow window as its central motif. It faces the magnificent gardens and is reminiscent more of an elegant country house than a royal palace in the heart of the city.

This lavish scheme was still incomplete at the time of the King's death in 1830 and a year later Nash was sacked for exceeding his budgets. The work was entrusted to Edward Blore, a more business-like but far less inspired architect. In general, he kept to the lines of Nash's design but made it more solid and less picturesque. The new king, William IV, had little interest in the building. He never lived there, and according to contemporary reports 'never calculated on the use of Buckingham Palace for any purposes of State'. Indeed, when the Houses of Parliament were burnt down in October 1834, the King offered the palace as a new home for Parliament, as a gift from the Crown. The offer, however, was declined, and William died in 1837, before Blore's work was completed.

There are some great and priceless works of art in the palace, but visitors cannot help but get the impression of wall-to-wall Hanoverians. William IV stares unblinkingly down from his gilt frame, while opposite is his Queen Consort, Adelaide of Saxe-Meiningen, the German princess he married to provide heirs for the Hanoverian line. Sadly, both their children died soon after birth, though previously William had fathered ten healthy illegitimate children with his mistress, the warm-hearted Mrs Jordan, an actress of some repute.

Unusually for a royal mistress, Mrs Jordan is commemorated. She and two of her children are represented in a sculpture, positioned in the lobby of the palace picture gallery. The group was commissioned by King William in 1834, 18 years after her death, as a romantic tribute to the woman with whom he was so happy. It was bequeathed to the Queen by the Earl of Munster, a descendant of the actress and the King, in 1975.

George V and Queen Mary, in 1914, by Solomon Joseph Solomon.

The Queen returns to Buckingham Palace after her Birthday Parade (Trooping the Colour) in June 1990.

King William's successor, the young Queen Victoria, took up residence in July 1837, when the palace was fresh from the builders. Nothing worked; it was too small, and the kitchens badly planned. She loved to dance, but none of the rooms was big enough for a court ball. Much more serious, after she married Prince Albert in 1840, was the absence of nurseries. The practical Victoria soon had these deficiencies put right and in 1851 built a new east range, designed by Blore, to close the forecourt and accommodate her large family. Marble Arch was then moved to its present site north of Hyde Park. The ballroom, built in 1853–5, was inaugurated in 1856 with a ball to celebrate the end of the Crimean War.

King George V and Queen Mary also put their stamp on the building, refacing the stucco façade in 1913 with an imposing design in Portland stone by Sir Aston Webb. The Queen took a keen interest in the improvement and restoration of the interior, banishing the traces of the Victorian era and reinstating much of Nash's original work. She left as a legacy to her succeeding custodians an informed and historically accurate approach.

During World War II the palace and its occupants became a symbol of defiance. It was bombed nine times, prompting Queen Elizabeth (now the Queen Mother) to make her most celebrated wartime response: 'I'm glad we've been bombed. It makes me feel I can look the East End in the face.'

The palace, of course, is still a great and mysterious symbol. That is why there is always a curious crowd outside, despite Her Majesty's decision seven years ago to lift part of the curtain.

The State Rooms of Buckingham Palace are open from early August to late September.

Clarence House

Across The Mall from St James's Park, almost hidden behind its garden wall, sits Clarence House, elegant in its exterior colour washes of dove grey and pale pearl. It is the London home of Queen Elizabeth, the Queen Mother, and on fine summer days passers-by, if they listen very intently, may just detect laughter, the hum of conversation and the chink of fine crystal and china coming from the other side of the wall. It is Queen Elizabeth indulging her passion for entertaining her guests in the open air. The table, dressed with flowers, will have been set beneath the trees, the hanging branches of which form what the hostess calls her *salles vertes*. Here in the sunshine, relaxed in the company of family and old friends, she holds court.

Clarence House has been the Queen Mother's town house since 1953, when she and Princess Margaret moved from Buckingham Palace and the new Queen and Prince Philip moved out. It was not the easiest of transitions, for there was some reluctance on both sides to the exchange. The Queen Mother, as she became after the death of George VI, had been the chatelaine of Buckingham Palace, a home packed with memories of her husband, for almost 15 years. Her elder daughter did not want to leave Clarence House, her first home as a bride, where she had been so happy. She was backed by Prince Philip. There was no practical reason, he said, why Clarence House should not be 'home' and Buckingham Palace 'the office'. But the Prime Minister, Winston Churchill, insisted: Buckingham Palace was a royal symbol and the Queen must live there. 'Now we've got to live behind railings', she declared, and almost five decades later, it is said, she still has little affection for the place.

The Queen Mother, however, over the years, settled happily into Clarence House, filling it with beautiful things, so that it is now a treasure-trove of exquisite furniture, paintings, china and sculpture. It has an

The Queen Mother at 90, in the grounds of Clarence House with her corgi, Ranger.

Lady Diana Spencer leaves Clarence House in the Glass Coach, for her wedding, almost disappearing beneath the billowing folds of her wedding gown of ivory taffeta and old lace.

agreeable sense of well-loved clutter, packed as it is with objects that tell the story of a life lived to the full. Family portraits and photographs are everywhere, mingling with sketches of the Queen Mother's beloved corgis, modern paintings and others by Millais and Monet, a model of Concorde and another of a jockey on a horse. Cupboards and wardrobes contain all the clothes she has ever worn in almost 80 years of public life, including her carefully preserved wedding dress. The contents of the house also reflect the story of the century; a century inextricably linked with the life of their owner, first as Lady Elizabeth Bowes-Lyon, then as Duchess of York, Queen Consort and, since 1952, Queen Elizabeth, the Queen Mother.

Clarence House is also a delightfully hospitable place, where guests are served the most generous gin and tonics in London! On 4 August each year it is the scene of a mix of carnival, street party and royal theatre. The Queen Mother's annual birthday 'parade' is beautifully stage-managed, and the

The King's Troop parade past the Queen Mother, watching with other members of the Royal Family, grouped at the main gates of Clarence House, on the occasion of Her Majesty's 99th birthday.

William IV, in 1837, by Sir David Wilkie. The portrait was painted in the year of the King's death.

Adelaide of Saxe-Coburg Meiningen, Queen Consort of William IV, in 1831 by Sir William Beechey.

birthday lady, who in other circumstances might have been an actress, knows how to work a crowd. Last year, as she embarked on her century, 5,000 people crowded round her front door, spilling out onto the pavements of The Mall. If she felt her age it rarely showed, and as she made her exit a young voice in the crowd shouted: 'Same time next year Ma'am.'

The then Lady Diana Spencer spent the night before her wedding at Clarence House. The noisy buzz from the crowds outside in The Mall disturbed her sleep and she woke early. Thereafter she was swept along on the momentum provided by a procession of arrivals: her hairdresser, make-up artist and the designers of her wedding dress, David and Elizabeth Emanuel, all on hand to assist in the transformation scene. As she walked down the staircase and climbed into the Glass Coach, used for most royal brides since 1911, her father, Earl Spencer, declared: 'Darling, I'm so proud of you.' Five years later Sarah Ferguson also left Clarence House in the Glass Coach for her marriage to the Duke of York.

Another bride associated with Clarence House is the Grand Duchess Marie, only daughter of the Emperor of Russia, who in 1874 married Prince Alfred, Duke of Edinburgh, Queen Victoria's second son. Prince Alfred, whose London residence it was from 1866 until his death in 1900, incorporated a Russian Orthodox chapel into the building for his wife's use.

Clarence House was built between 1825 and 1828 for William, Duke of Clarence, later William IV. Previously he had lived in apartments on the site, cohabiting with the actress Dorothea Jordan, who bore him ten children. The couple eventually separated, and in 1814 Mrs Jordan fled across the Channel to escape her creditors. She died two years later and in 1818 William married a German princess, Adelaide of Saxe-Meiningen. The couple needed a larger, grander home, and so in 1824 John Nash was commissioned to redesign and remodel the apartments to create Clarence House. Work began the following year; it was finally finished, late and desperately over-budget, in 1828, but William and Adelaide continued to live there when they became King and Queen in 1830.

When the King died in 1837, the house became the home of his sister Princess Augusta. Then in 1841 the Duchess of Kent, Queen Victoria's mother, most unhappily was moved there, away from the centre of power at Buckingham Palace. After her death it was successively the London residence of the Duke of Edinburgh and then of his brother the Duke of Connaught, Queen Victoria's third son. He died in 1942, when it briefly became the wartime headquarters of the Red Cross and the St John Ambulance Brigade.

Clarence House is never open to the public.

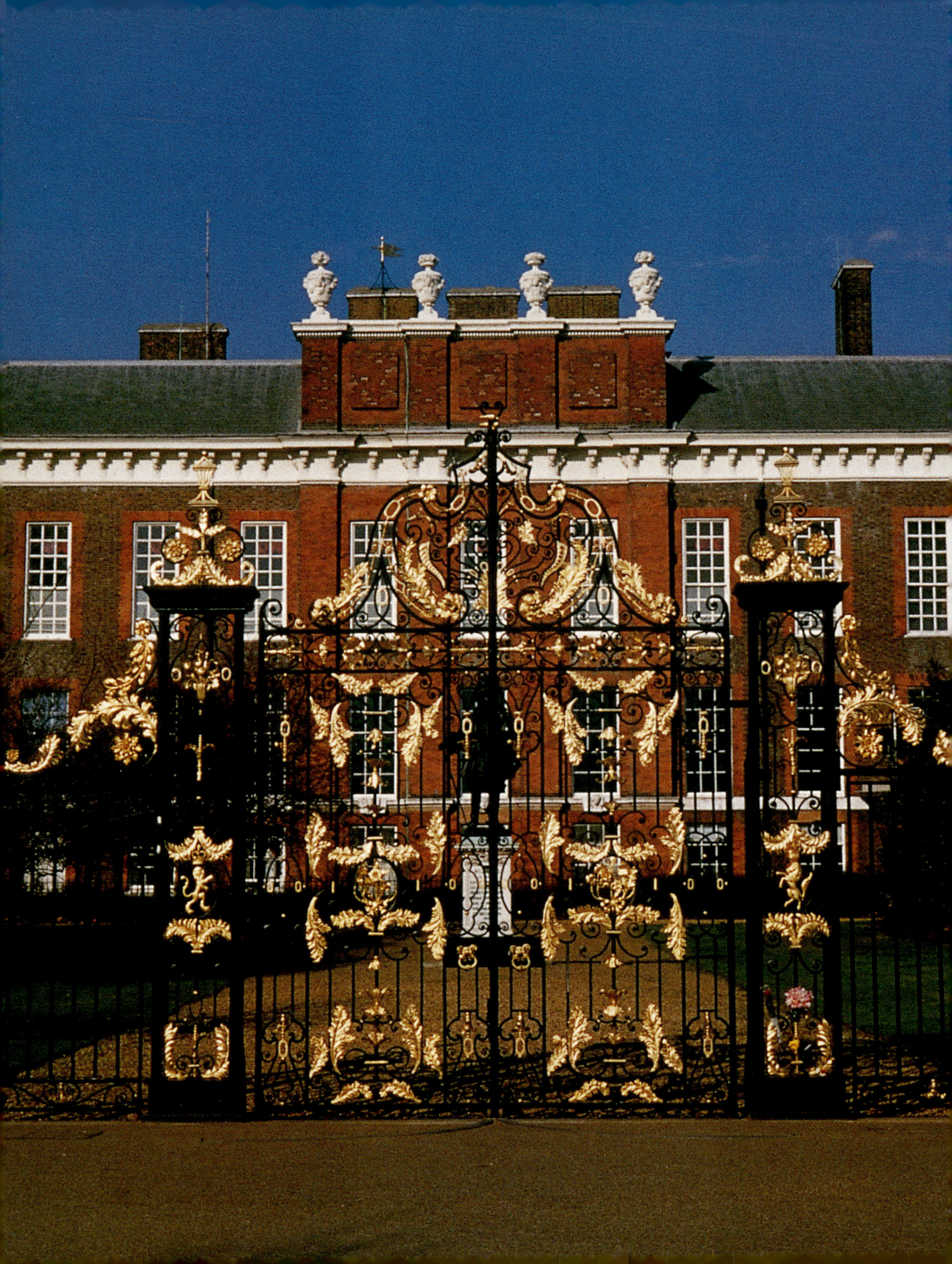

Kensington Palace

Kensington Palace, set in the rural illusion created by Kensington Gardens, has the image of a royal village. It all started soon after William of Orange and his wife, Mary, the elder daughter of the deposed King James II, came to the throne in 1689 and found living in the Palace of Whitehall, the official residence of the Tudor and Stuart monarchs, uncongenial. William suffered from chronic asthma, and damp, rambling Whitehall, set beside the River Thames, did nothing to improve his condition. Queen Mary found the palace oppressive, and in a letter complained to the King about how much she felt shut in there, adding: 'a poor body like me, who has been for so long condemned to this place, … sees nothing but water or wall.'

So there was really nothing for it but to move, and towards the end of February 1689 the Oranges decamped to Hampton Court and began the search for a house in a healthy location that would also be near the seat of government at Westminster. In the summer of 1689 they found Nottingham House (a modest mansion by Jacobean standards), owned by the King's Secretary of State, the Earl of Nottingham, standing in Kensington, a village that 'esteem'd a very good Air'. The King and Queen paid £20,000 for their rural hideaway, which according to the historian John Bowack, writing in the early 18th century, was 'the only retreat near London he (the King) was pleas'd with'.

Facing page: the ornate gates at the south front of Kensington Palace.

The Earl of Nottingham, owner of Nottingham House, in the village of Kensington. William III bought the house as an escape from polluted Whitehall Palace and set about enlarging and improving the new royal home.

Kensington Palace from the south in the early 18th century. The Orangery, to the north was built for Queen Anne and is now a public restaurant.

Kensington Palace in 1730, in the reign of George II.

William III and Mary II a fanciful study of the joint sovereigns on horseback by Adam-Francois van der Meulen.

The King set Christopher Wren to work to enlarge and improve the new royal home, with Nicholas Hawksmoor as Clerk of Works. The Queen, installed in temporary quarters in nearby Holland House, was impatient to move in and often drove to Kensington to chivvy the workmen. The Court was installed shortly before Christmas that year, though the house was still far from finished.

Kensington House, as Nottingham House was renamed, was thereafter the favoured residence of successive sovereigns. In its early days it was more like a private country house than a royal palace, but after extensive and expensive changes it was transformed into a grander place altogether, though still fairly modest for a royal residence in the age of Louis XIV. It became known as Kensington Palace and during the tenure of William and Mary's successor, Queen Anne, was the setting for the first intimate links between the Royal Family and the Spencers, the family of Diana, Princess of Wales.

The centre of power, the palace also became a hub of intrigue and patronage, dominated by the close friendship between the Queen and Princess Diana's ancestress the formidable Sarah Churchill, Duchess of Marlborough. These two remarkable women, in effect, ruled the land and were companions for 26 years, but it was a bickering, love-hate relationship. Their quarrels often

The statue of William III, set outside the south front of the Palace. Cast in bronze, it was the work of Heinrich Baucke. According to its inscription it was 'presented (in 1907) by William II, German Emperor and King of Prussia to King Edward VII for the British Nation'.

Queen Mary II's bedchamber. She died there in 1694 of smallpox, aged only 32.

Queen Anne by Sir Godfrey Kneller.

had a political dimension, and the acrimony echoed around the galleries and closets of the palace where Princess Diana and the Prince of Wales, almost 280 years later, were to have their London home. The final bitter quarrel came in 1710, after which the Duchess was forced to surrender her keys of office as Keeper of the Privy Purse. The two women never spoke again, and Queen Anne died at Kensington Palace four years later, a cripple, tortured by gout and arthritis, and worn out by the 17 pregnancies she endured in the hopeless effort to provide England with an English king.

Queen Anne was a Stuart to her fingertips and, it was said, she would have wished to make her Roman Catholic half-brother James Stuart her heir. Instead, the succession went to the great-grandson of James I, the Protestant Prince George, Elector of Hanover, who moved into Kensington Palace with his German mistress, whom he created Duchess of Kendal. George I left his wife, the tragic Sophia Dorothea of Luneburg-Celle, behind in Germany, where he had had her imprisoned for infidelity and, it was rumoured, arranged to have her lover murdered.

The King liked Kensington Palace because it reminded him of his palace at Herrenhausen in Hanover. He built the east front with three new State Rooms from 1718 to 1722, and commissioned William Kent to paint the Grand Staircase with images of members of the court, including a pathetic creature called Peter the Wild Boy, who had been found in the woods near Hamelin, in Hanover. Peter was brought to England and allowed to roam on all fours, like a bizarre animal, in the

George I. Studio of Sir Godfrey Kneller.

The King's Gallery, built for William III in 1695, was redesigned and redecorated for George I. In 1835 it was partitioned into a suite of rooms for the Duchess of Kent and Princess Alexandrina Victoria, who professed herself to be very pleased with the conversion. In 1994 the King's Gallery was refurbished in the decorative style created for George I by William Kent in 1725.

palace grounds, living off moss and grass, and 'displaying the agility of a squirrel'. He resisted attempts to civilise him, and outlived the King by nearly 60 years.

King George II made Kensington Palace one of his main residences, spending between four and six months of the year there. His Queen, Caroline of Brandenburg-Anspach, a very keen gardener, opened the gardens to the more respectable public, and the Broad Walk, now frequented by rollerbladers, joggers and strollers, became the resort of fashion and a Saturday promenade for high society. The Queen was also instrumental in the creation of the Round Pond, the Serpentine, and its upper reach, the Long Water. An urn commemorating her transformation scene overlooks the Serpentine.

The Queen died in 1737 and on her deathbed begged the King to remarry, only to receive the reply, somewhat lacking in gallantry: 'No, I shall have mistresses.' The palace had been ruled by Queen Caroline and now it was dominated by her ghost. The King missed his wife much more than he anticipated, and large parts of the palace fell into disuse. He too died there, in 1760, expiring somewhat ingloriously in a small chamber next to his water closet.

His grandson and successor George III showed little interest in the palace, and the building took on a forsaken air. The new King took his court to St James's Palace and bought Buckingham House, at the top of The Mall, for use as a private family home. Kensington Palace fell into disrepair, but at the end of the 18th century and the beginning of the 19th, separate households became necessary for some of the King's 15 children and other members of the Royal Family. Substantial alterations, costing £600,000, a vast amount of money in those days, were carried out to accommodate them, prompting an outburst from the Duke of Wellington who described the numerous royal relatives as 'the damnedest millstone about the necks of any government that can be imagined'.

The King's fourth son, Prince Edward, Duke of Kent, brought his pregnant Duchess to set up home in Kensington Palace, and on 24 May 1819 Princess Alexandrina Victoria was born there. The Duke did not, however, enjoy paternity for very long, as he died in 1820. A warm-hearted, lively and mischievous child, the Princess mixed little with other children and in later years recalled her early childhood at Kensington as 'rather melancholy'. When her governess, Baroness Lehzen, told her, early in 1830, that she might be Queen since neither her uncle George IV (then but a few months from death) nor his brother the Duke of Clarence (later William IV) had any surviving legitimate children, her characteristic reply was: 'I will be good.'

William IV died in the early hours of 20 June 1837 and the Princess became Queen. The news was broken to her by the Archbishop of Canterbury and the Lord Chamberlain, who drove at speed in a landau with four horses from Windsor to Kensington. On arriving at about 5 o'clock, they had to knock, thump and ring for a long time before they could rouse the porter at the gate. Eventually the 18-year-old Queen was summoned and received them in one of the lower rooms, still wearing her nightgown, and with tears in her eyes, but according to a contemporary account 'perfectly collected and dignified'. The Queen attended her Accession Council that morning at 11 o'clock, in the Red Saloon, and the following day, after her proclamation at St James's Palace, moved into Buckingham Palace with her mother.

George II by Christian Frederick Zincke.

Caroline of Anspach, when Princess of Wales, by Sir Godfrey Kneller.

The Duchess of Kent and Princess Alexandrina Victoria.

31

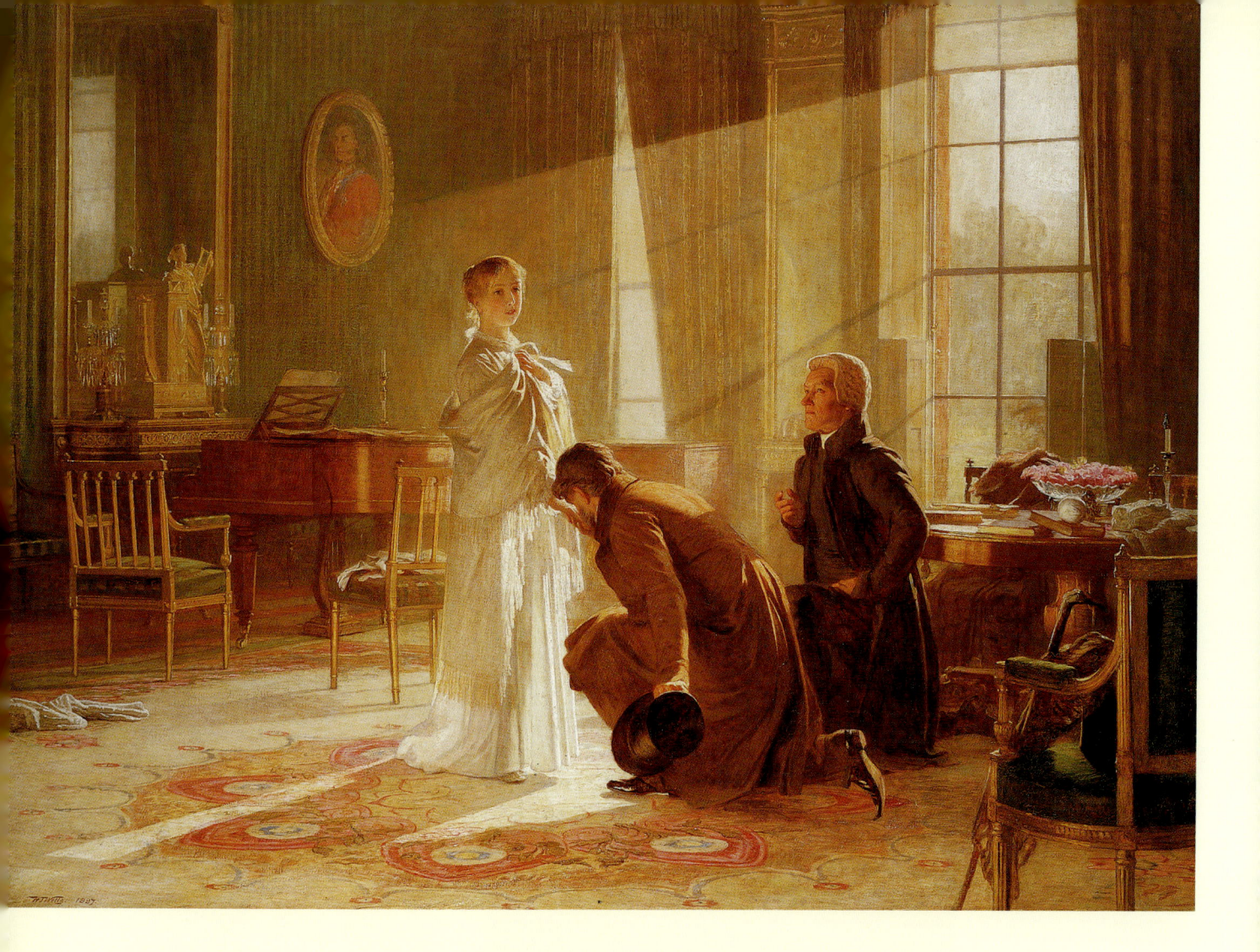

Victoria Regina by Henry Tamworth Wells. The Archbishop of Canterbury and the Lord Chamberlain announce to Princess Alexandrina Victoria that she is Queen.

In the years that followed Queen Victoria strenuously resisted suggestions that her old home should be demolished (one suggestion was that it should become the site of the National Gallery), and instead began installing royal, and some (relatively) poor relations in its apartments. The rooms she once occupied with her mother were allocated to the Duke and Duchess of Teck. Their first child, Victoria Mary, married the future King George V and took great interest in the arrangement of the palace after it was opened to the public in 1899. Queen Victoria went to inspect the restoration of the State Apartments on 15 May that year. It was her last visit to Kensington Palace.

Her grandson George V once expressed a wish to pull down Buckingham Palace, which he never liked, and use the money to rebuild Kensington Palace, making it the main town residence of the sovereign, but this remained an unfulfilled dream. The continuing use of the palace to house elderly royal relatives prompted Edward VIII to christen it 'the aunt heap', while the latter day tabloid press coined their own name for it: 'Coronet Street'. Princess Alice, Countess of Athlone, the last of Queen Victoria's grandchildren, lived there until she died, aged 97, in 1981. This redoubtable princess, daughter of Prince Leopold and Princess Helen of Waldeck-Pyrmont, was celebrated locally as 'the grand old lady of Kensington' and insisted on catching the number 9 bus rather than use an official car. On most days she would go out to buy a bouquet from her friend Ada Shakespeare, who sold flowers in Kensington High Street.

Princess Louise, Marchioness of Lorne, the sixth child of Queen Victoria and Albert, the Prince Consort. A talented sculptor, she had her own studio in Kensington Palace and exhibited at the Royal Academy. Her statue of her mother wearing her coronation regalia is set outside the Palace.

Queen Victoria by Princess Louise.

A more leisured age. A promenade in the sun along the banks of the Long Water.

Today the palace is home to a different generation, and in court parlance is known simply as 'KP'. Princess Margaret lives in 1a Clock Court, once home to Princess Louise, Queen Victoria's sculptress daughter (her most famous work, a marble statue of her mother as a young Queen, stands outside the east front of the palace), and the Prince and Princess of Wales lived in apartments 8 and 9, successfully merged into one by government architects. Following the death of the Princess the rooms were cleared and there appear to be no plans to install new occupants.

The Waleses' immediate neighbours were Prince and Princess Michael of Kent, while the Duke and Duchess of Gloucester, and the Duke's mother, Princess Alice, Duchess of Gloucester, who was born on Christmas day 1901, also have their home in this royal condominium. The Duke and Duchess of Kent are the latest residents of 'KP'. In 1997 they moved into Wren House, which began life in the 1690s as part of a stable block built to house the mounts of the Horse Guards, but which is now a handsome residence in its own right.

The only parts of Kensington Palace open to the public are the State Apartments and the Royal Ceremonial Dress Collection. The exhibition recently included an evocative display of some of the evening gowns worn both publicly and privately by Diana, Princess of Wales.

33

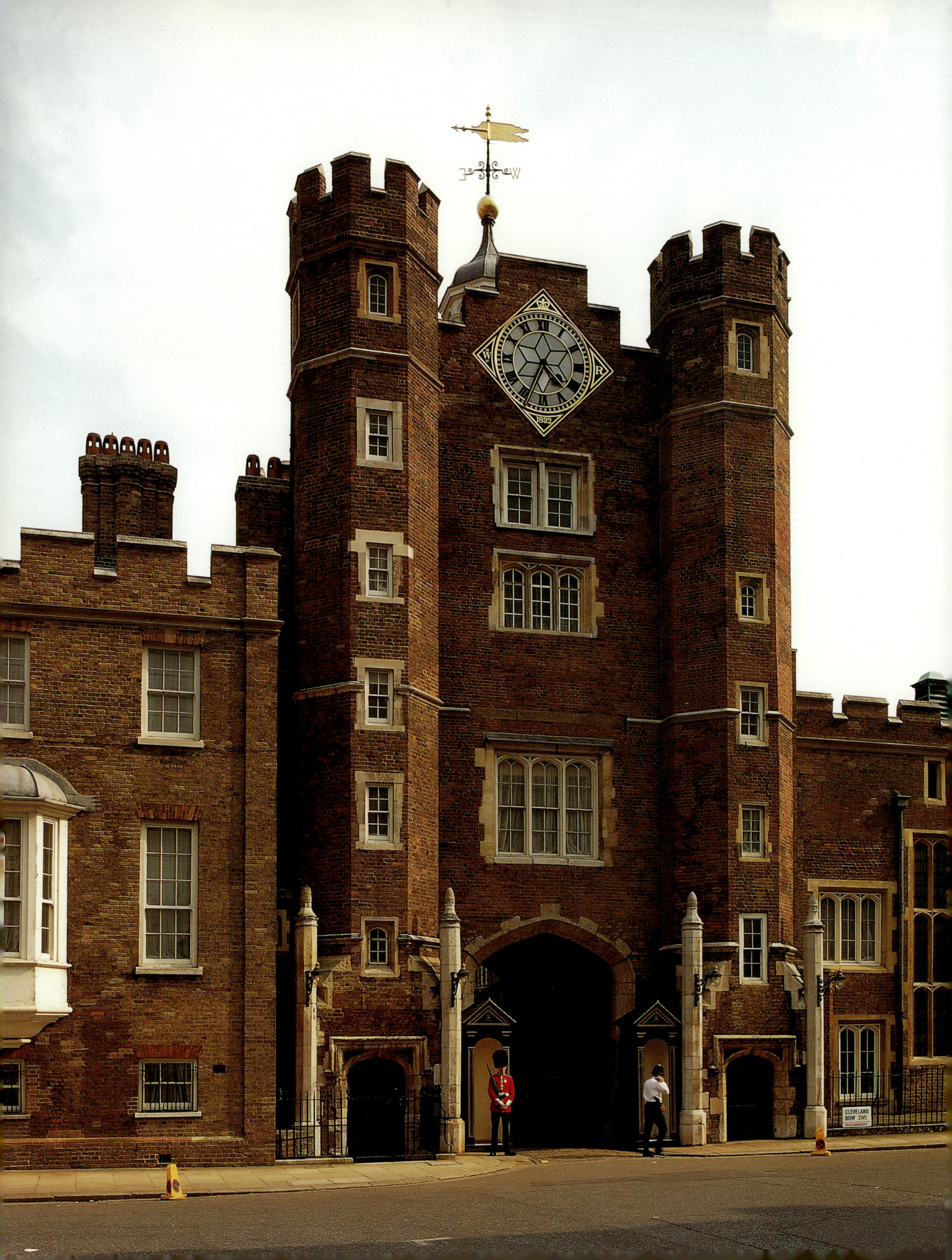
1832
CLEVELAND ROW SW1

St James's Palace

Across from St James's Park can be glimpsed the castellated walls, turrets and towers of St James's Palace, the senior palace of the Sovereign, and still the 'Court' to which foreign ambassadors and high commissioners are accredited.

The palace was built by Henry VIII from 1532 on the site of the leper hospital of St James the Less, in red brick with blue diapering, and was the principal royal residence from 1698, when Whitehall Palace was burnt down, until 1809, when it too was largely destroyed by fire. Opposite Friary Court, where the proclamation of a new Sovereign takes place, is the Queen's Chapel, by Inigo Jones, which has the distinction of being the first church in England to be built in the style of the Italian High Renaissance. It was begun in 1623 for the forthcoming wedding of Charles I and the Infanta of Spain, which never took place, and was completed for the arrival of Queen Henrietta Maria.

The palace also includes the Chapel Royal, where on 30 January 1649 Charles received the sacrament of Holy Communion before crossing St James's Park to his execution in front of the Banqueting House in Whitehall. It was a freezing morning and the King wore two shirts to prevent himself shivering, lest he should give his enemies the impression he feared the fate awaiting him. Princess Diana's coffin rested in the Chapel Royal before her funeral on 6 September 1997.

Henry VIII by an unknown artist.

Charles I on his way to execution. The King wears his Garter Star, the most ancient order of chivalry.

Facing page: the Tudor gatehouse of St James's Palace.

35

Mary I, by Master John.

Elizabeth I in her coronation robes by an unknown artist.

Within the palace are magnificent State Apartments and a warren of 'Grace and Favour' residences occupied by members of the Royal Household. The offices of the Prince of Wales (and at one time Princess Diana), the Duke and Duchess of Kent, Princess Alexandra, the Marshal of the Diplomatic Corps, the Central Chancery of the Orders of Knighthood, and that of Her Majesty's Representative at Ascot are also there, as well as the headquarters of the Yeoman of the Guard (not to be confused with the Yeoman Warders who guard the Tower of London), the Gentleman at Arms, the Royal Watermen and the Royal Collection.

The Prince of Wales and his sons, Princes William and Harry, now have their London home in York House, on the north side of Ambassadors' Court, one of the four courts around which the palace buildings sprawl. They occupy the rooms once lived in by the Duke and Duchess of Kent, who have moved to Wren House, in Kensington Palace. York House was also the home of another Prince of Wales, who in his youth seduced Britain and the Empire with his charm and then, as Edward VIII, relinquished his crown in order to marry the twice-divorced American socialite Wallis Simpson. In January 1936 he joined Mrs Simpson at a window of the palace Guard Room to watch Garter King of Arms proclaim his accession.

St James's Palace has, over the centuries, seen a succession of royal inhabitants, living out their domestic and social lives while also playing their part in some of the more famous events in history. Henry VIII used the tennis court sited on the area north-east of the great Tudor Gatehouse. Anne Boleyn stayed the night after her coronation and again following the birth of an unwanted princess, later Queen Elizabeth I. She was eventually discarded by the King, but the initials 'HA' entwined in a lovers' knot, discernible on two fireplaces in the State Apartments, recall the his once great passion for the woman who supplanted his first wife, the long-suffering Catherine of Aragon. It was in St James's Palace, in 1558, that Henry and Catherine's daughter Queen Mary signed the treaty surrendering Calais, Britain's last French possession. The unhappy Queen declared that when she died the name of Calais would be found stamped on her heart.

Mary's half-sister Elizabeth I was in residence at the time of the threat to her realm by the Spanish Armada and set out from St James's to rally the troops assembled at Tilbury against the Duke of Parma. The future Charles II and James II were both born and baptised at St James's, as were James's daughters, Mary of York (later Queen Mary) and Anne of York (Queen Anne), and his son, Prince James Francis Edward Stuart, who was acknowledged by the Jacobites as James III but dismissed

Charles II in 1665 by John Michael Wright.

St James's Palace in the 18th century.

by supporters of the Hanoverian dynasty as the Old Pretender.

George II preferred Hanover and Kensington and only lived at St James's when he had to. His absences prompted a wit to scrawl on the palace walls in 1736: 'Lost or strayed out of this house, a man who has left a wife and six children on the parish.' Four of the sons of George III were provided with homes within the palace walls, including Frederick, Duke of York, who was given Godolphin House (now Lancaster House, which can also be seen from the Memorial Walk) and William, Duke of Clarence, who was given Clarence House. As William IV, he was the last sovereign to use St James's as a residence, but after his death in 1837 court functions, such as balls, drawing rooms and royal weddings (Queen Victoria's was one such occasion) continued to be held there. Court levées were held at St James's up to 1939, but now the State Apartments are used for official, but much less formal and elaborate, entertaining.

St James's Palace is not open to the public.

KENSINGTON
GARDENS

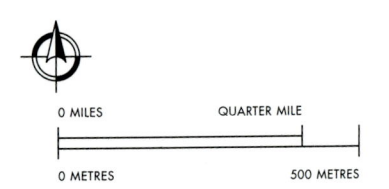

HYDE PARK

0 MILES QUARTER MILE

0 METRES 500 METRES

The Diana, Princess of Wales Memorial Walk

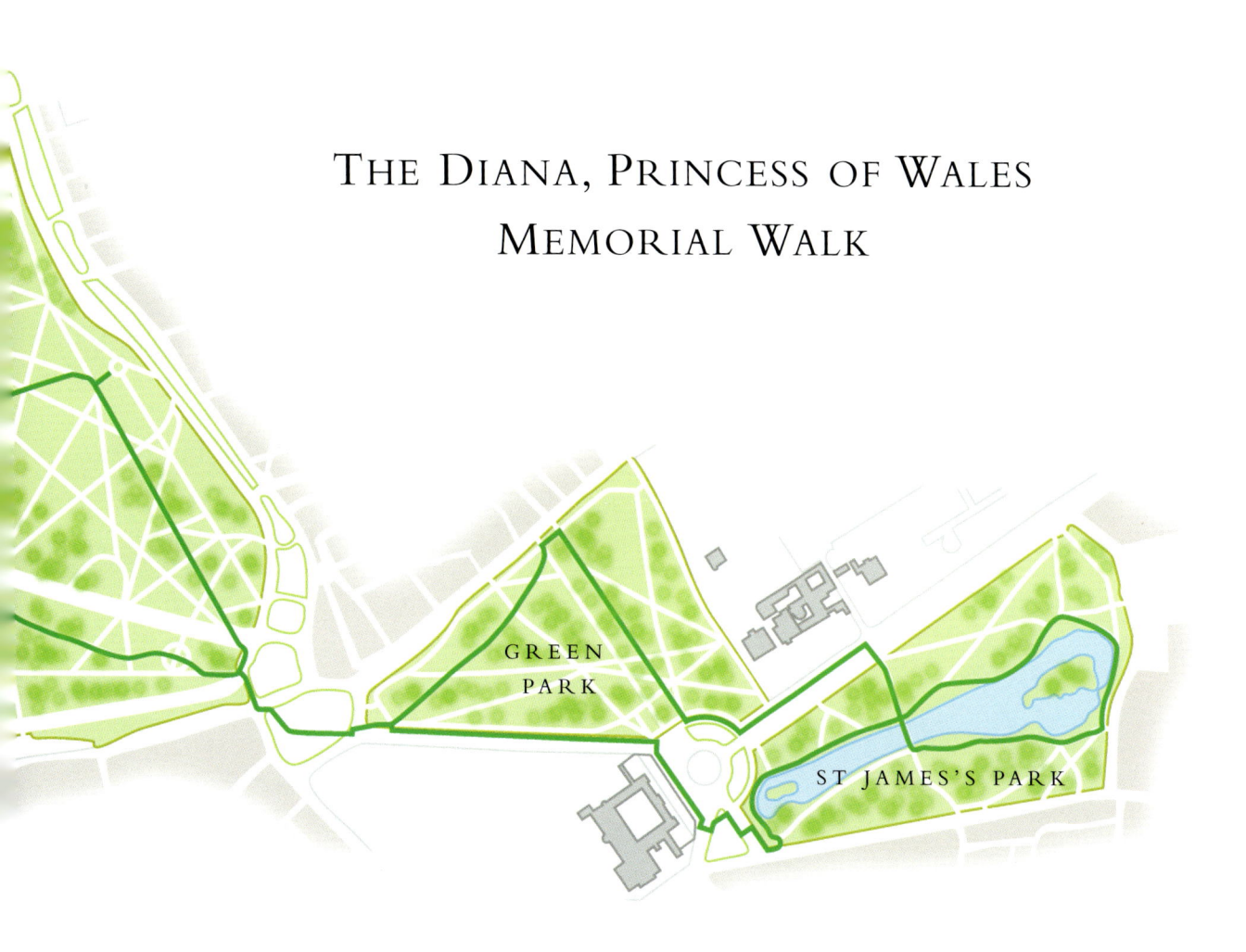

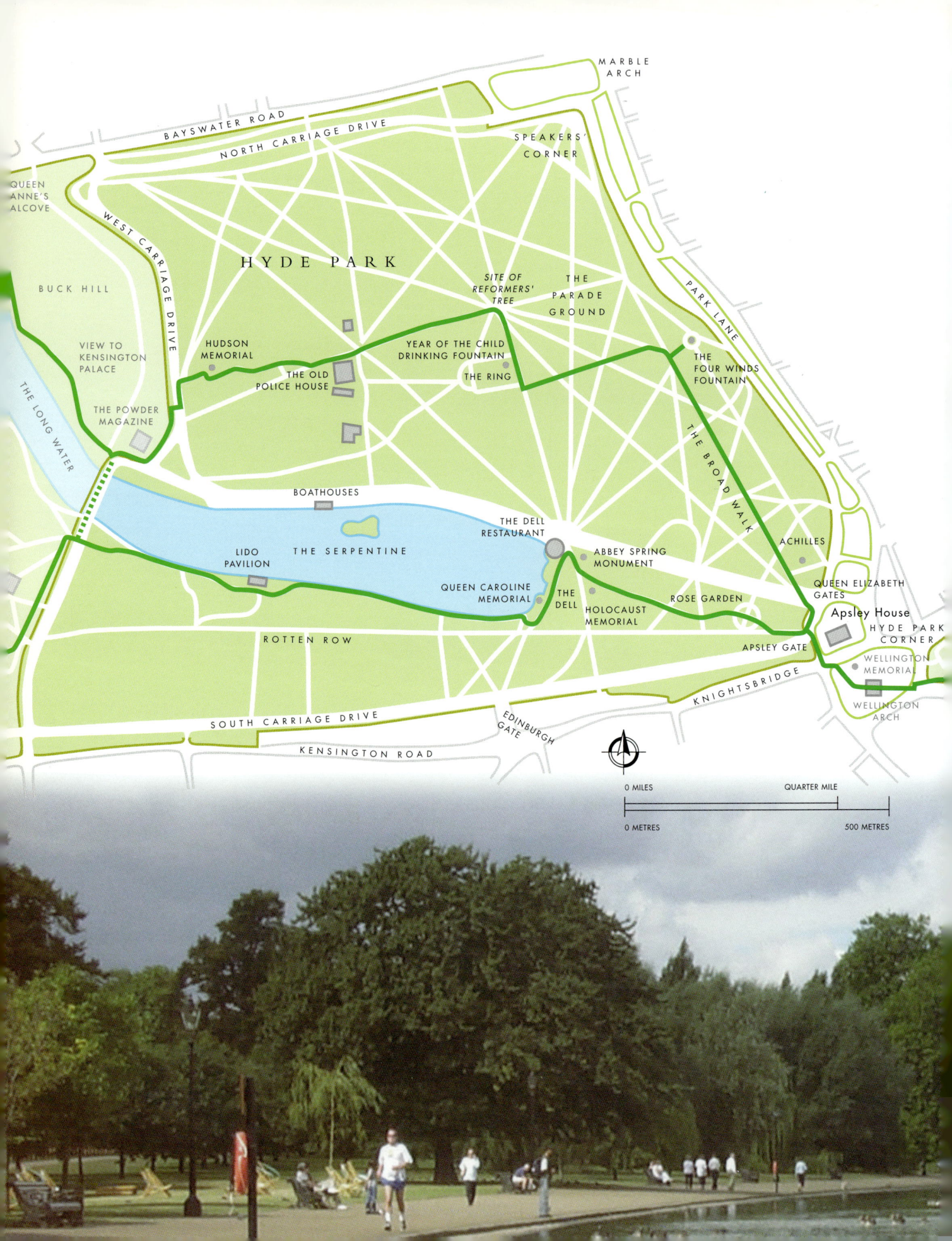

HYDE PARK

- MARBLE ARCH
- BAYSWATER ROAD
- NORTH CARRIAGE DRIVE
- SPEAKERS' CORNER
- QUEEN ANNE'S ALCOVE
- WEST CARRIAGE DRIVE
- BUCK HILL
- VIEW TO KENSINGTON PALACE
- THE POWDER MAGAZINE
- THE LONG WATER
- HUDSON MEMORIAL
- THE OLD POLICE HOUSE
- SITE OF REFORMERS' TREE
- THE PARADE GROUND
- YEAR OF THE CHILD DRINKING FOUNTAIN
- THE RING
- PARK LANE
- THE FOUR WINDS FOUNTAIN
- THE BROAD WALK
- BOATHOUSES
- THE SERPENTINE
- THE DELL RESTAURANT
- LIDO PAVILION
- QUEEN CAROLINE MEMORIAL
- THE DELL
- ABBEY SPRING MONUMENT
- HOLOCAUST MEMORIAL
- ROSE GARDEN
- ACHILLES
- QUEEN ELIZABETH GATES
- Apsley House
- HYDE PARK CORNER
- APSLEY GATE
- WELLINGTON MEMORIAL
- WELLINGTON ARCH
- ROTTEN ROW
- SOUTH CARRIAGE DRIVE
- EDINBURGH GATE
- KNIGHTSBRIDGE
- KENSINGTON ROAD

0 MILES — QUARTER MILE
0 METRES — 500 METRES

Hyde Park

*L*IKE the other Royal Parks in London Hyde Park owes its existence to Henry VIII, who acquired vast tracts of land in the 1530s to satisfy his love of the chase. The King wanted to create a hunting ground that stretched from his palace at Whitehall to the slopes of Hampstead. Present-day St James's Park, Regent's Park and Hyde Park are the result. These particular acres were once farmed by the monks of Westminster and included a series of fishponds along the Westbourne river.

The parks were enclosed, stocked and kept strictly private. In a proclamation of 1536 Henry stated: 'As the King's most royal Majesty is desirous to have the games of hare, partridge, pheasant and heron preserved, in and about the honour of his palace of Westminster, for his own disport and pastime, no person, on the pain of imprisonment of their bodies, and further punishment at his Majesty's will and pleasure, is to presume to hunt or hawk, from the palace of Westminster … to Hampstead Heath.' Hunting, as well as providing fresh meat, was seen as the sport of kings and a form of corporate entertainment. In 1592 Queen Elizabeth and the Duke of Anjou, one of her many unsuccessful suitors, watched the hunt from stands in Hyde Park.

Over the centuries the royal prerogative was whittled away until, in the 19th century, the parks became the popular recreation grounds we know today. In Hyde Park the process began in 1630 when Charles I opened it to the public and laid out the Ring, a carriageway or racecourse north of the present Serpentine boathouses. Under Charles II the park, walled and restocked, became a fashionable venue and the *beau*

The Hyde Park Screen by Decimus Burton forms a backdrop to the carriages of the fashionable, c1825

Achilles

Prince of Wales Gate Lodge

monde, even the King himself, could be seen there daily, circling the Ring in their splendid carriages or showing off their latest finery. The diarist Samuel Pepys, ever conscious of his social position, wrote in 1668: 'Took up my wife and Deb, and to the Park, where being in a hackney (hired coach) and they undressed, was ashamed to go into the Tour, but went around the Park, and so with pleasure home.'

By the 1730s, however, the smart set had tired of the Ring and the park, despite the occasional highwayman, had become a popular public resort. Among its attractions were riding, swimming, duelling and, most thrilling of all, executions. This gruesome entertainment came to an end in 1783, when the last public hanging took place at Tyburn, on the north side of the park. By the early 19th century the park was in a deplorable state and in 1823 the Commissioners of Woods and Forests took matters in hand with a programme of improvements. Policing, along with regular closing hours, was introduced and the architect Decimus Burton, aged only 25, was appointed to deal with the structure of the park. By putting up new railings and building gates and lodges in a neo-classical style, he gave it dignity and a unified character.

The Hyde Park section of the walk is best entered from Hyde Park Corner, through Apsley Gate, the elegant Greek Revival screen of 1825 that was the culmination of Burton's work for the park. It combines an Ionic colonnade with a frieze copied directly from the Parthenon sculpture. At this period Burton was also designing a new western approach to Buckingham Palace, the gate of which formed the beginning of a route that would run through his own Constitution Arch – which then stood in line with the screen – to end at John Nash's Marble Arch in the forecourt of the palace. Along with Apsley House and St George's Hospital (now the Lanesborough Hotel), the gate and arch made a very fine group of neo-classical monuments at one of the main entrances to London. Now, unfortunately, its significance is lost in the maze and roar of traffic.

Hyde Park Corner Screen (Apsley Gate)

Apsley House, whose postal address is simply Number 1, London, was the home of the Duke of Wellington. One of the final honours enjoyed by the Duke was to be Ranger of the Metropolitan Royal Parks. The house, built by Robert Adam in 1771–8, was enlarged in the 1820s and faced in yellow Bath stone. Inside is a vast, nude statue of Napoleon by Canova,

Apsley House, Number 1, London

while outside, to the north, is an even larger one of Wellington himself by Richard Westmacott. Erected in 1822 it was the park's first statue, and its most controversial. Loosely described as Achilles, the huge figure was cast in bronze obtained from cannon captured in Wellington's campaigns. The image was taken from a Roman group on Monte Cavallo but the head was clearly modelled on the Duke himself. This was a problem, for a statue that was also nude. The Ladies of England, who had commissioned it, were horrified but the press was delighted. The offensive member, however, was soon covered by a small fig leaf.

Queen Elizabeth Gates

Beside the *Achilles* statue are the Queen Elizabeth Gates, another controversial addition to the park. They were installed in 1993 in honour of the Queen Mother. The central screen, by David Wynne, unites the lion of England and the unicorn of Scotland. The gates themselves are in stainless steel patinated with natural oxides. Their sculptor, Giusseppe Lund, designed them to be 'feminine and fresh with the charm of an English garden', in deliberate contrast to the formal, masculine character of their setting, but they attracted much public criticism. The former Arts Minister Lord St John of Fawsley sprang to their defence, saying: 'The gates are full of joy, strength and courage like the great personage in whose honour they have been created. … Mr Lund is greatly to be congratulated on his imagination, creative powers and the sheer technical control of his material. He deserves and will gain the nation's gratitude.'

From here the route goes north, along the Broad Walk magnificently flanked by rows of plane trees. On the left, just in front of the private gate into the shrubbery, is an unusual tree, *Cladrastis lutea*, also known as Kentucky yellow wood since its timber

Blossom time in Hyde Park

Kentucky yellow wood (*Cladrastis lutea*)

Four Winds fountain

turns yellow. Further up the Broad Walk on the right is the *Four Winds* fountain sometimes known as the *Joy of Life* fountain. Dating from 1963, when Park Lane was widened, its gravity-defying bronze figures were sculpted by T. B. Huxley-Jones. In Victorian times there was a much admired sunken garden here, on the site of an old reservoir that once provided the royal palaces with water. Behind the fountain can be seen the imposing towers of the Dorchester Hotel, the headquarters of General Eisenhower in World War II.

Turning left after the fountain, towards a small building flanked by trees, the route crosses the Parade Ground. It has served as an English *champ de Mars* for 400 years, since the days when Queen Elizabeth held the first military reviews in the park. Gun salutes are still fired here on royal anniversaries. The building is a rather stylish, porticoed public lavatory, one of the many built in the 1900s. Beside it is a drinking fountain by Theo Crosby for the 1981 Year of the Child, when 180,000 children attended the Great Children's Party. It was erected as a tribute to the park staff, who surely deserved it. Behind is the Lookout Environment Centre, which offers children the opportunity to study animal and plant life in the park. There are plans to turn the adjoining reservoir area, on the site of the long-vanished Ring, into special habitat.

Year of the Child drinking fountain

To the north is the site of the Reformers' Tree, marked by a circular mosaic pavement. In the mid-19th century there were frequent, and sometimes violent, public demonstrations in the park attracting vast crowds. In 1866, when the Commissioner of the Police refused the Reform League permission to hold another mass rally, enraged protesters tore down the iron railings, swarmed in and burnt down a venerable tree. The subsequent rioting and bloodshed persuaded the authorities that a stick-and-carrot approach was called for. The police presence was increased, but Speakers' Corner was sanctioned in 1871 as a public meeting place. Close to Marble Arch, at the other side of the Parade Ground, it is still a powerful symbol of the British right to free speech. Hyde Park continues to attract protestors, and more than 100,000 members of the Countryside Alliance gathered here without incident in 1997.

The Reformers' Tree sculpture was unveiled by Tony Benn MP in July 2000 and celebrates the right of public assembly

The Hyde Park riots of 1866

The Old Police House, to the west on the left of the route, was built in 1900–02 on the site of the Magazine Barracks. A fine Queen Anne revival building, it is the headquarters of the Royal Parks Agency and the Royal Parks Constabulary, which are now responsible for keeping order in the park. The path then follows the line of

The Old Police House

Small Copper butterfly

Rima The Hudson Memorial

The Meadow

the shrubbery to the Hudson Memorial, passing the Chinese evergreen magnolia (*Magnolia delavayi*), a small tree with huge leaves that are among the largest found outdoors in the British Isles. In late summer it has wonderfully scented, parchment-coloured flowers.

The memorial to the writer and naturalist W. H. Hudson is tucked into the bird sanctuary to the south of the nursery area. Hudson grew up on a ranch in Argentina but spent most of his life in London, often in great poverty. He was probably the first person to appreciate that the growth of London was having an adverse effect on its bird life. In his *Birds of London* of 1898 he attacked the Parks authorities for their 'improving spirit which makes for prettiness' but provided no shelter for wildlife. He called for parks where trees were 'not deprived of their lower branches, nor otherwise mutilated, or cut down because they were aged or draped in ivy', nor were the 'wind-chased yellow and russet leaves that give a characteristic beauty (to be) ... removed like offensive objects', nor 'the native shrubs and evergreens ... to be replaced by that always inharmonious exotic, the rhododendron'. A sanctuary, he said, could be made in any park with 'a small pond, with or without islets, with sedge, rushes, and a few shrubs or willows on its margins for cover, the whole protected from dogs and people by a light iron fence'.

At the time Hudson was dismissed as a charlatan, but his views eventually won respect and the authorities are now very keen to encourage wildlife. Although most of the park is taken up by open grassland and widely spaced trees which provide little natural cover, an area to the north is now treated as meadow and only mown once a year, in the late summer. The cuttings are left on the ground for a short while, and as a result the range of grasses and flora has increased. Grasshoppers and small moths have colonised the area, though butterflies are still scarce. Shrubberies encourage songbirds, and the area around the Hudson Memorial is treated as natural woodland, with native and non-native species and dense undergrowth. On rotten wood around the Lookout area stag beetles have been found.

As well as common birds such as robins, wrens, blue tits and greenfinches, a number of more unusual species breed in the park, including the tawny owl, mistle thrush, blackcap, coal tit, nuthatch, treecreeper, chaffinch and spotted flycatcher. Although it is more difficult to lure mammals back into the park, a fox is said to inhabit the Hyde Park corner shrubbery and two species of bat, the pipistrelle and the noctule, feed by the Serpentine, though their roosts have not been found. Hedgehogs are also occasionally seen.

The memorial itself is not an unqualified success, as the stone sides of the pool are too steep to allow birds to drink or bathe. Like other monuments in the parks, it also attracted the wrath of the public when it was unveiled by the Prime Minister, Stanley Baldwin, in 1925. It was the relief carving by Jacob Epstein, showing Rima, the spirit of the forest in Hudson's celebrated book *Green Mansions*, that caused such offence. 'Take this horror out of the park!' shrieked the *Daily Mail*. 'It would be a reproach to all concerned if future generations were allowed to imagine that this piece of artistic anarchy in any way reflects the spirit of the age,' intoned various dignitaries. A journalist wrote caustically, 'The large eagle-like bird in the sculpture must be a portrait statue of old Hudson himself. When I used to … lunch with him at Whiteley's, it was like taking one of the hunched eagles at the zoo out of his cage for an airing.' Fortunately, good sense prevailed in the end. George Bernard Shaw, Sybil Thorndike and Augustus John lent their names to a letter in *The Times*; the artist Muirhead Bone argued their case with the Commissioner of Works; and the memorial stayed. It is now considered one of Epstein's finest early works.

Beyond the Hudson Memorial is the West Carriage Drive, which marks the boundary with Kensington Gardens. Turning left, the Serpentine Bridge is reached. At this point there is a choice of either following the route around Kensington Gardens, which is described on pages 53–65, or completing the Hyde Park loop by walking along the south bank of the Serpentine.

The bridge is a convenient place to pause and look at the Long Water, winding up through Kensington Gardens, and the Serpentine, stretching down towards Hyde Park Corner. In the distance can be seen the Palace of Westminster. Once this was the focal point of a landscape that seemed entirely natural, but the view is now marred by the high-rise buildings that dominate the skyline.

The Serpentine Bridge

This vista is the result of the first – and only – major landscaping in the park. It took place in the 1730s when Queen Caroline, the dynamic German wife of George II, oversaw the development of Kensington Gardens and used the existing string of fishponds to create the Serpentine and the Long Water. It is said that she had grandiose plans to build a new palace and turn virtually the whole of Hyde Park into a private demesne, but Walpole, the Prime Minister, squashed her proposals by saying it would cost her merely 'three crowns'. The Hanoverian dynasty that had recently succeeded to the crowns of England, Scotland and Ireland could not afford to alienate its subjects.

Queen Caroline's great-grandson, the hopelessly extravagant Prince Regent, decided in 1814 to woo the public with a vast fair in premature celebration of Napoleon's defeat. Its climax was a mock naval battle on the Serpentine in which the miniature French fleet was set alight. This event, as well as costing the Government the outrageous sum of £40,000, caused considerable damage to the park and gave rise to the 1823 programme of improvements. Alongside the work undertaken by Decimus Burton, the circulation was improved by John Loudon McAdam, the inventor of the 'macadam' road surface. He made new rides and built the Serpentine Bridge, to an elegant design by George and John Rennie, to link the new, smart residential areas of Bayswater to the north and Knightsbridge to the south. Previously a small cascade had marked the junction between the two lakes; the bridge created a thoroughfare that quite changed the character of the park.

After crossing the bridge, the route leads to the Lido Pavilion, built in 1930 to provide the mixed bathing and sunbathing facilities demanded by the Sunlight League. Lord Lansbury, the First Commissioner of Works, was keen to improve recreational facilities during the Depression years and had appealed for funds. The pavilion was built with the help of £5,000 donated by a Mr D'Arcy Cooper in memory of his son, whose death in World War I is commemorated by a plaque by the entrance. Beyond it is Beach Head, with its diving platform and swimming area. Members of the Serpentine Swimming Club have swum here daily, winter and summer, since 1864. Boating is also popular and the Royal Thames Yacht Club's annual regatta takes place in February.

The shore on the far side of the Serpentine is popular for roller-blading. There are two boathouses, the one to the right erected in 1903, near the former Receiving

Mock naval battle on the Serpentine, 1814

The Lido Pavilion

The Serpentine

House that belonged to the Royal Humane Society. This institution was founded in 1774 to provide a rescue service for the Serpentine, which has always been a magnet for drunks, revellers and suicides. On a dark December day in 1816 Harriet Shelley, the estranged wife of the poet, drowned herself in the Long Water.

Away to the right the Knightsbridge Barracks can be seen. An unfortunate example of Brutalism in architecture, the barracks were built in 1967–9 by Sir Basil Spence for the Household Cavalry. With their tall bearskins, jangling spurs and shining boots, the men are a magnificent sight as they leave the yard under the watchful eye of the police. The troupes of children in yellow jumpers and brown breeches that congregate under the trees come from nearby Hill House School, which Prince Charles briefly attended as a small boy.

At the end of the Serpentine the route turns left over a bridge, passing an elegant urn in memory of Queen Caroline. The canopied Dell Restaurant at the end was designed by Patrick Gwynne in 1965 and is one of the few modern buildings in the Royal Parks of true architectural merit. There is a long tradition of refreshment here. In 1668 Samuel Pepys, after another minor embarrassment, resorted to the Lodge to drink 'a cup of new milk' before returning home. In the 19th century, however, the provision of food became a contentious issue. In 1883 the deeply conservative Duke of Cambridge, who had succeeded the Duke of Wellington as Ranger, wrote 'I have … set my face against the erection of any places for Refreshment in the Royal Parks, as I consider that these Parks are for the enjoyment of fresh air, and are not to be turned into Tea Gardens.' He was gently overruled.

Opposite the entrance to the restaurant is the Abbey Spring Monument (1868), an urn marking the ancient spring that supplied water to Westminster Abbey. The right to use this water, granted by Edward the Confessor, was jealously guarded until the conduit was cut off by the Metropolitan Railway in 1861. Here the route goes right and then left, towards the Rose Garden. The area below the bridge is known as the Dell and contains a megalith. This incongruous assembly is all that remains of the 1861 drinking fountain that was constructed from stones quarried at Liskeard in Cornwall.

The Dell has been planted with shrubs and exotic trees very different from the parkland species – lime, plane, oak and horse chestnut – that predominate elsewhere in the park. They include the Caucasian wingnut (*Pterocarya fraxinifolia*), which has striking flowers in the summer in the form of long yellow-green tassels, a vigorously growing dawn redwood (*Metasequoia glyptostroboides*), a magnificent weeping beech (*Fagus sylvatica* 'Pendula') and a *Magnolia* x *soulangeana*. Throughout this area there are also choice birch trees, including the white-stemmed Himalayan birch (*Betula utilis*) and the striking red-barked birch (*B. albosinensis* f. *septentrionalis*). Many of these are grouped around the Holocaust Memorial, a dignified tribute to the right of the path that leads to the Rose Garden. A little further along to the left can be seen another interesting tree, the Caucasian elm (*Zelkova carpinifolia*), with its brush-shaped crown and muscular trunk.

In the Rose Garden there is a statue by Countess Feodora Gleichen of *Diana* (1906), drawing her bow along the tunnel of pleached lime, and a *Boy and Dolphin* by Alexander Munro (1862). This was once the centrepiece of the Victorian sunken garden that was demolished to make way for Park Lane.

To the right is Rotten Row, which was created by William III to link Whitehall with his new palace at Kensington. Illuminated by 300 lanterns to discourage footpads, it was the first road in England to be lit in the hours of darkness and was called the *route du roi*, a name that was corrupted over the years to Rotten Row. The road soon became as fashionable as the Ring had once been, though other than the Hereditary Grand Falconer, only royalty was allowed to drive there. It remained a very smart place to ride, so much so that in 1908 Edward VII issued a letter to the effect that 'ladies who ride astride in the Park will not be allowed to come to court.' A century later sartorial, and equestrian, standards have declined, but on a lucky day one can still see the Queen's immaculate carriages taking the air.

The Holocaust Memorial

Diana

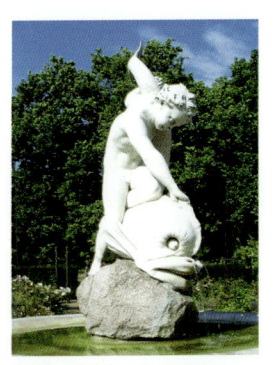

Boy and Dolphin fountain

The Dell

Rotten Row

Bluebells in Hyde Park

KENSINGTON GARDENS

- Black Lion Gate
- Bayswater Road
- Marlborough Gate
- North Carriage Drive
- The Diana, Princess of Wales Memorial Playground
- The Italian Gardens
- Queen Anne's Alcove
- West Carriage Drive
- Hyde Park
- Buck Hill
- Peter Pan
- View to Kensington Palace
- Site of 'Seeming Mount'
- Physical Energy
- The Long Water
- Hudson Memorial
- The Orangery
- Queen's Temple
- The Powder Magazine
- Kensington Palace
- Queen Victoria Statue
- The Broad Walk
- The Round Pond
- Serpentine Gallery
- The Serpentine
- Lido Pavilion
- Bandstand
- The Mount
- St Govor's Well
- Rotten R[ow]
- Esme Percy Memorial
- Flower Walk
- Queen's Gate
- The Albert Memorial
- Coalbrookdale Gates
- South Carriage Dri[ve]
- Palace Gate
- Kensington Road

0 MILES — QUARTER MILE
0 METRES — 500 METRES

Kensington Gardens

*I*T IS often thought that the boundary between Hyde Park and Kensington Gardens is marked by the Long Water, but in fact it is defined by the West Carriage Drive. The route enters the Gardens through a gate just beside the Serpentine Bridge and continues up the Peacock Walk. To the right is the Powder Magazine, which was built in 1805 and remodelled in the 1820s, probably by Decimus Burton. It later became a tearoom and is now the Park Office.

The Powder Magazine

Half-way up the Long Water, with the gentle slopes of Buck Hill on the right, is an opening in the lakeside vegetation. It reveals Kensington Palace in the distance and also the temple that was built for Queen Caroline by William Kent in 1734–5 as part of the scheme to create the Long Water and the Serpentine.

On each side of this lawn the banks of the Long Water have been developed as a wildlife sanctuary, with tangled undergrowth, hollow trees and carefully placed nesting boxes to provide shelter for birds and mammals. Boats are not allowed on the Long Water, which makes it a haven for waterfowl, and the ubiquitous Canada geese are discouraged by the management's furtive practice of pricking their eggs. As a result Kensington Gardens has a far greater variety of birds than Hyde Park. Great crested grebe, mute swan, mallard, pochard, tufted duck, coot and moorhen breed on the lake, which is also the home of three-spined sticklebacks, roach, gudgeon and eels. Other

The Long Water

The Italian Gardens

nesting birds include the mistle thrush, four varieties of tit, the treecreeper and the great spotted woodpecker. Near by, an area of Buck Hill is treated as a meadow. It is cut in the spring and then left to grow until September, which gives a sward of fine grasses and encourages meadow buttercups and daisies.

At the head of the Long Water are the Italian Gardens, constructed in 1860–61, when the Westbourne river was cut off and a new well sunk to supply the park with water. The Italianate loggia doubles as a pumphouse and behind it lie the arched remains of a former head wall outlet. The Italian Gardens are a reminder that Kensington Gardens is effectively a 'layered' landscape, in which the early Georgian formal garden is overlaid with the decorative features of a Victorian public park. Here the architectural character of the Italian Gardens conflicts with their pastoral setting, but despite this they remain a popular attraction, particularly in summer, when the splashing fountains are refreshing.

On the east side of the gardens is a stone bench marking the site of St Agnes's well, once thought to cure eye troubles, but which dried up in 1861. Near by is a statue of Edward Jenner, the country doctor who developed the smallpox vaccine. It was sculpted by William Calder-Marshall and originally placed in Trafalgar Square. Despite Jenner's fame, this was considered too grand a position and in 1862 the statue was moved. *Punch* commented on its demotion:

> England, ingratitude still blots
> The escutcheon of the brave and free;
> I saved you many million spots,
> And now you grudge one spot to me.

Edward Jenner

Medlar (*Mespilus germanica*)

Queen Anne's Alcove

To the rear of the gardens is Queen Anne's Alcove, a fine piece of classicism by Christopher Wren. It was made in 1705 for the formal garden south of Kensington Palace, but was moved to its present position in 1867, because it was considered unsightly and a resort for undesirable persons. Around it are a number of notable trees. A medlar tree (*Mespilus germanica*) with its spreading, twiggy crown can be seen to the right of the path leading to Lancaster Gate. Its delicate flowers are followed by strange fruit which, once 'bletted' or frosted, make a fine jelly. Beside the entrance to the public lavatory is a dawn redwood (*Metasequoia glyptostroboides*) and at the beginning of the North Flower Walk a Chinese privet (*Ligustrum lucidum*).

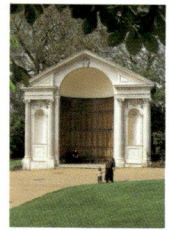

At the north-west corner of the Italian Gardens, among the trees, there is the *Two Bears* drinking fountain by Kenneth Keeble-Smith. It was positioned to mark the 80th anniversary of the Metropolitan Drinking Fountain Association, a worthy institution founded in 1859 as an alternative to the commercial water companies. Its aim was to combat cholera, which was then plaguing the city, as well as the traditional scourge of drunkenness. In the 19th century, when the parks were heavily used by the public, it was very necessary to provide clean drinking water. Without it, the children would be seen 'flocking around the cabstand, and drinking with the horses out of their pails'.

On the west bank of the Long Water is a swamp cypress (*Taxodium distichum*), a striking deciduous tree that was introduced into Britain from the New World around 1640 by John Tradescant. Very old specimens develop root growths that protrude jaggedly from the waterline like a medieval *cheval-de-frise* to act as breathing organs and stabilisers in wet ground.

Two Bears drinking fountain

A little further on is the *Peter Pan* statue. Designed by Sir George Frampton and paid for by J. M. Barrie, it was erected in 1912 and immediately voted the most beautiful of London's statues. The model is usually said to have been Nina Boucicault, who played Peter Pan in 1904, but the sculpture may instead have been based on Barrie's photographs of his little friend Michael Llewelyn Davies in fancy dress. Although Kensington Gardens were immortalised by Peter Pan, not everyone approved of the phenomenon. The avant-garde artist and writer Wyndham Lewis complained that the 'sickly and dismal spirit of that terrible key-book … has sunk into every tissue of the social life of England'. The plaque in front of the statue was unveiled in 1997 by Princess Margaret, who made friends with Barrie during her third

Peter Pan

Peter Pan detail

birthday party. He was then a neighbour of her grandparents in Scotland.

Shortly after the statue the route turns right and heads for the vast *Physical Energy* statue. It passes some ancient sweet chestnut trees (*Castanea sativa*) with their deeply furrowed bark. They are survivors of the early 18th-century landscaping of Kensington Gardens and harbour beetles that are regarded as indicators of ancient woodland.

The statue is by George Frederick Watts OM. Its history dates back to 1870, when Watts made an equestrian monument to an ancestor of the Duke of Westminster. In 1902 he was invited to make one cast as a memorial to Cecil Rhodes in Cape Town and another for Kensington Gardens. He explained the concept as 'a symbol of that restless physical impulse to seek the still unachieved in the domain of material things …. This is a symbol of something done for the time, while the rider looks out for the next thing to do.' However incoherent, this statement does suggest that the work is an expression of a particularly dynamic era.

One senses a clearer purpose behind the beautiful Queen's Temple, which can now be seen from the rear between the statue and the Serpentine Gallery. It seems rather isolated in the expanse of open parkland. Originally it was less exposed and, like Kent's other garden buildings, was intended to give visual focus and an Arcadian spirit to a carefully contrived view. In 1835 the Temple narrowly escaped being turned into a 'Mohammedan' summerhouse and later it was enlarged to provide accommodation for the labourers' foreman. It has since been restored to its original form.

Physical Energy

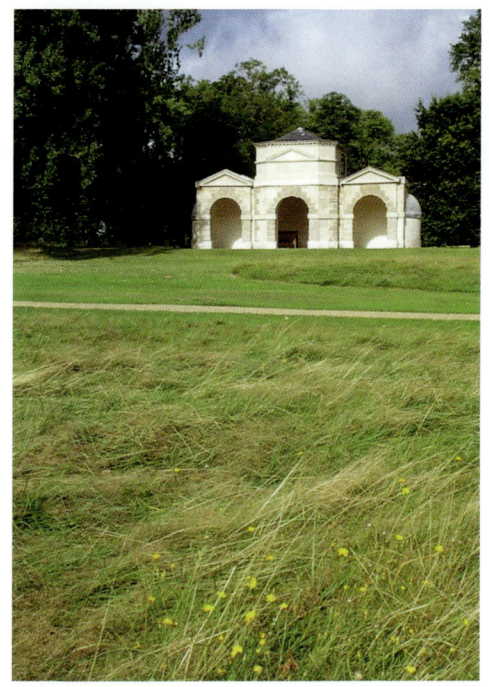

The Queen's Temple

56

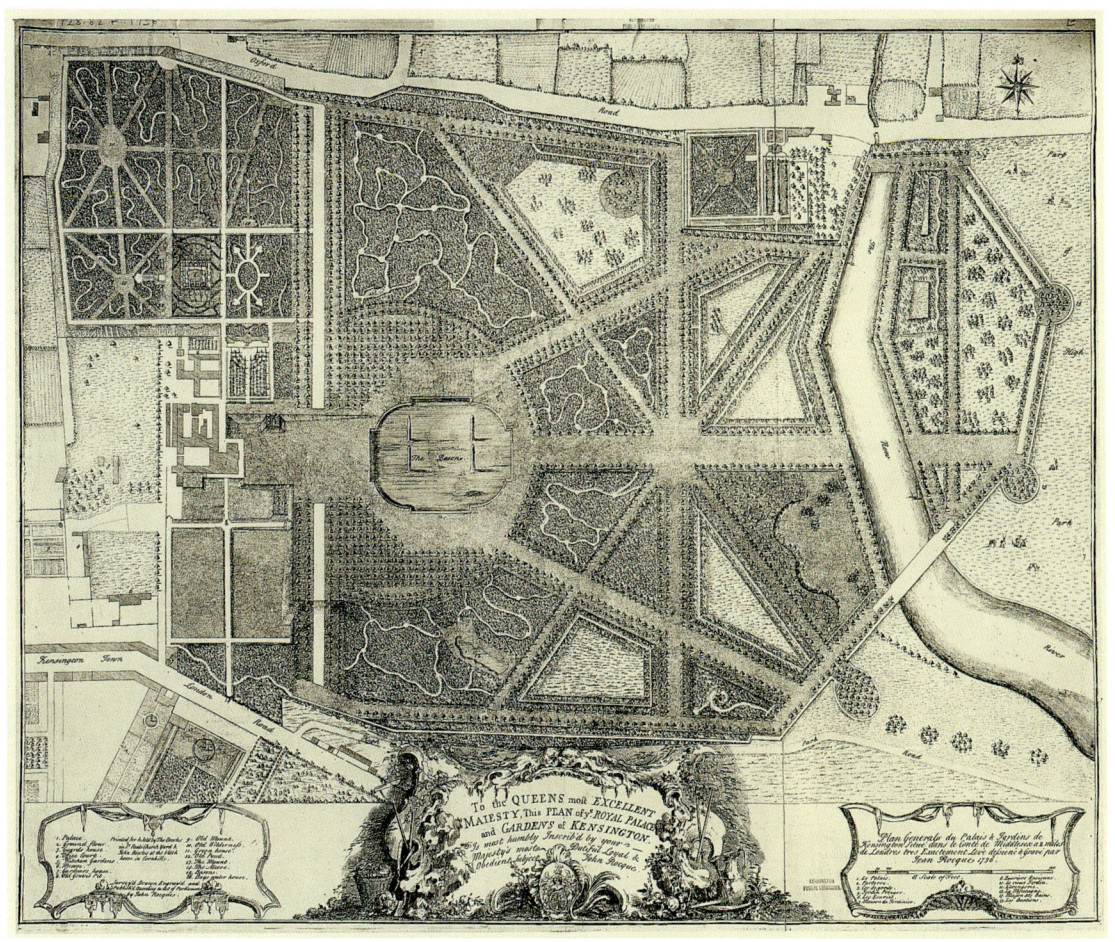

Plan of Kensington Gardens, dated 1736, by Jean Rocque illustrating Bridgeman's scheme

The colossal horse, with the Albert Memorial glinting in the distance, makes a convenient point to consider the landscaping undertaken in 1726–35 by Queen Caroline when she created the Long Water and the Serpentine. The design was largely the work of the Royal Gardener, Charles Bridgeman, who planted the paddock that was originally here with a *patte d'oie*, or goosefoot, of radiating, tree-lined *allées* and secondary cross-avenues. Within it were paths framed by lime espaliers, serpentine walks, woodland borders and open lawns, the whole forming a garden full of variety and surprise for visitors. Its focal point was the Round Pond in front of the palace, while beyond the Long Water, at the far side of Buck Hill, Bridgeman built a bastioned ha-ha, or concealed ditch, to separate the private royal garden from the wild, and public, expanses of Hyde Park.

The less formal aspects of the scheme reflect in some way William Kent's involvement, since he

The Round Pond

was not only an architect but also an influential garden designer. Described as 'the inventor of an art that realises painting, and improves nature', he 'leaped the fence, and saw that all nature was a garden'. At Kensington Gardens he is said to have planted dead trees to 'give a greater air of truth to the scene'. One of Kent's maxims was that 'Nature abhors a straight line.' Hence, the newly formed Serpentine and Long Water had gently curving sides, a departure from the perfectly rectangular watercourses fashionable in the past. It is true that they do not curve very much, but from the ground the illusion is sufficient.

When the Queen died in 1737 work on the garden stopped. Her husband, George II, was shocked to discover she had spent over £20,000 of Treasury money on the alterations: he had assumed she was paying for them herself. On his death in 1760 the palace ceased to be a royal residence, and by the 1780s much of the Queen's garden had been destroyed. Later it was grazed by sheep.

From *Physical Energy* the route heads for the Round Pond and turns right, picking up the line of the Great Bow. This was planted by Bridgeman as a double arc of trees to give a sense of enclosure to the pond. Over the years, as trees died and were replaced at random, the lines of the Great Bow were lost, but it has now been replanted with lime trees.

The path leaves the Great Bow Walk and heads for the Diana, Princess of Wales Memorial Playground. The first playground on this site was constructed in 1909 and the first swings were the gift of J. M. Barrie, who lived near by in an elegant Regency house on Bayswater Road. Beside it is the *Time Flies* drinking fountain, given in the same year by a Mrs Galpin. Its cosy design and stern reminder of passing time evoke those vanished Edwardian childhoods when nannies to the nobility had their own benches and Peter Pan lived in the gardens but 'the children never caught a glimpse of him.' The *Elfin Oak*, populated by tiny gnomes, was added in 1930, the result of Lord Lansbury's appeal to improve facilities in the Royal Parks. The 800-year-old tree trunk came from Richmond Park and the sculpture was by Ivor Innes. Recently the playground has been redesigned as a memorial to Diana, Princess of Wales. A naturalistic playground with a loose Peter Pan theme, it has a pirate ship, sandy beach, wigwam camp and mermaid fountain, in which children are encouraged to 'go native', however wet and mucky this may be.

Kensington Gardens c1905, the nannies' rendezvous

Time Flies clock tower and drinking fountain

KENSINGTON GARDENS

The Diana, Princess of Wales Memorial Playground

On the palace side of the playground is the site of the Seeming Mount. The ground, now used for football and *t'ai chi*, is flat but the mount was a visual trick created by trees of different heights. It was part of the garden scheme instigated by Queen Anne and devised by Henry Wise, Bridgeman's predecessor as Royal Gardener, in 1704–5. This whole area to the north of the palace had been a gravel pit, but Wise planted it as wilderness with 'antique Busts and Statues very well placed at the end of the little walks'. The Seeming Mount formed part of this Wilderness, as did

The Orangery

the sunken garden by the Orangery. The Queen also planted a new formal garden to the south of the palace and appropriated 100 acres from Hyde Park to make a paddock for deer. All this has disappeared, though evidence of the former paths was discovered during archaeological investigations carried out before the reconstruction of the playground. Only the splendid Orangery remains as Queen Anne's most important legacy to the gardens. Built in 1704–5 for summer supper parties, it was designed by Hawksmoor but altered by Vanbrugh.

There are some unusual trees in this area, a date plum (*Diospyros lotus*), with its shiny pointed leaves, at the corner of the Orangery and, just in front of it, an euodia (*Tetradium daniellii*). On the lawn between the Orangery and the Broad Walk there is a black walnut (*Juglans nigra*) and a paulownia (*Pawlownia tomentosa*), which has spectacular, foxglove-like flowers in early spring. On the other side of the hedge is a handsome topiary garden that provides a perfect formal setting for the Orangery. Further along, beside the Broad Walk, is a sunken garden that recalls the one planted for Queen Anne but which was laid out in 1908–9 in the manner of the Tudor garden at Hampton Court.

In front of Kensington Palace is a marble statue of Queen Victoria by her daughter Princess Louise. Though erected in 1893, it shows the Queen at her coronation. She sits, very solemn, sceptre in hand, facing the Round Pond that once housed George I's 'tortoises' or turtles. Beside it, he had a 'snailery' and near by a tiger's den. Now noisy swans and geese parade the pond's shallow banks, while model boats float gently over its surface.

The flat expanse of lawn to the south of the palace was once William and Mary's Dutch-style garden. A visitor reported in 1691 that

Queen Victoria sculpted by Princess Louise

The Broad Walk

The Bandstand

'Kensington Gardens are not great, nor abounding with fine plants. The orange, lemon and myrtles with other trees they had there in summer were all removed to Mr. London and Mr. Wise's greenhouse at Brompton Park, a little mile from here. But the walks and grass are laid very fine, and they are digging up a flat of four or five acres to enlarge their garden.' Henry Wise, as well as being Royal Gardener, was a partner in England's first professional nursery. Thirteen years later, when Queen Anne uprooted this garden, Wise was appointed to give it a more English aspect – no doubt, to the benefit of his nursery. The Broad Walk, which runs past the south garden to terminate at Palace Gate, was planted by Bridgeman. Its original elms were replaced in 1954 with limes and maples following the first outbreak of Dutch elm disease. Along the Kensington Road fence are a number of Indian horse chestnuts (*Aesculus indica*), which are more elegant than their European cousins, with whiter flowers and finer leaves.

To the left of the Broad Walk is the bandstand. Along with St Govor's well, which marks the site of an ancient spring thought to have healing properties, and the Esmé Percy Memorial, the doggy fountain at the end of the Flower Walk, it indicates the changing character of the gardens from an aristocratic enclave to a public recreation ground. In the early 19th century, when the

St Govor's Well

Esmé Percy Memorial

The Albert Memorial

gardens were first opened to the general populace, there was mounting pressure to create municipal parks in Britain. The urban population was growing at an alarming rate, conditions in the cities were miserable and insanitary, and there was a real fear of social unrest. The Royal Parks were among the few green spaces available to Londoners, but they were totally lacking in any facilities. Following the example of the new municipal parks, they then took on an increasingly complex role. Fresh air and gentle exercise were no longer sufficient: the public was also to be educated, improved and entertained. This necessitated horticultural displays, bandstands, boathouses, sports pavilions, drinking fountains, memorials and uplifting statuary.

Like any change, it challenged established attitudes. In 1855 Queen Victoria, by giving permission for music to be played in the gardens for the first time, unwittingly created a public uproar. The Archbishop of Canterbury objected to the music and the Keeper of the Privy Purse agreed. The latter, though believing that the 'recreation and amusement of the class who are confined during the week is of great importance', did not think 'military music a necessary ingredient of it'. The Queen rescinded her permission and the first bandstand, near Mount Gate, was not erected until 1869.

The Flower Walk was planted in 1843 and includes many rare trees and shrubs. Starting from the west end, they include a shapely evergreen called *Osmanthus heterophyllus*, a Chinese persimmon (*Diospyros kaki*) which has edible fruits, another date plum, a cork oak (*Quercus suber*) and the Californian laurel, or headache tree (*Umbellularia californica*). One sniff of its leaves will cause a dreadful headache. The route, however, passes to the south of the Flower Walk, offering a magnificent view of the Albert Memorial framed by stately plane trees. This is a semi-woodland area, full of blossom and bulbs in spring, and just off the route is a Persian ironwood tree (*Parrottia persica*) with shedding, pale brown bark. It can be seen on the left, where a small path cuts through to the Flower Walk.

To the right can be seen Queen's Gate which was erected in 1858 to provide access for the new, exclusive residences across the road. It has recently been repainted in its original red colour. The stags on the pillars, positioned in 1919, were the gift of a local vintner but were cast in Paris by Val d'Osne and may have come from another site. Beside the gates is one of Decimus Burton's elegant lodges.

The last, and greatest, monument in the Gardens is the Albert Memorial, erected in 1864–72 to commemorate the Prince Consort, who had died of typhoid in 1862. It was funded by public subscription as 'a tribute of … gratitude for a life devoted to the public good', though in truth Queen Victoria's earnest, cultivated German husband had never been much liked in Britain. Its designer, George Gilbert Scott, envisaged the memorial as 'a kind of ciborium … on the principle of the ancient shrines … to protect a statue of the Prince. These shrines were models of ancient buildings, and my idea was to realise one of these imaginary structures with its precious metals, its inlaying,

Queen's Gate

its enamels, etc.' The statue of the Prince, seated and holding the Great Exhibition catalogue, was by J.H. Foley. Its original heavy gilding was painted black during World War I to escape the attention of hostile Zeppelins but was restored in the 1990s in a massive conservation programme undertaken by English Heritage.

One of the Prince's greatest achievements was the Great Exhibition. It was held in 1851 on flat ground south of the Serpentine in the Crystal Palace, a vast glass conservatory designed by Joseph Paxton, superintendent of the Duke of Devonshire's gardens. The exhibition, which attracted six million visitors, was one of the highpoints of the Victorian age – Queen Victoria described its opening as 'the greatest day in our history'. Afterwards the building was removed to Sydenham, where it burnt down in 1936. The money raised by the exhibition funded the purchase of the land on which were built the scientific and cultural institutions for which South Kensington is famous. These include the Victoria and Albert Museum, the Science Museum, the Royal College of Music, the Imperial College of Science and Technology, the Natural History Museum and the Royal Albert Hall.

Europa The Albert Memorial

The statue itself forms the centrepiece of an elaborate sculptural programme that reflects the Prince's diverse interests and virtues. Around the base are the four Continents that contributed to the Great Exhibition. Above, on the podium, are the Industrial Arts: Agriculture, Manufacture, Commerce and Engineering. The frieze, one of the masterpieces of Victorian sculpture, depicts the Western cultural tradition in a procession of poets, musicians, artists and architects. At the corners of the shrine stand the Greater Sciences – Geometry and Physiology, Astronomy and Rhetoric, etc. – while the Virtues and Angels bring it to a glorious conclusion. The work of many artists, it remains a permanent witness to the dynamism and assurance of the Victorian age.

At the end of Albert Memorial Road are the Coalbrookdale Gates, designed by Charles Crookes for the Great Exhibition and cast in one piece at Coalbrookdale. They were moved to their present position in 1871 as part of the scheme for the memorial. Their finials, supporting a crown, represent Peace, while the stag's head vases evoke the origins of the park.

Beyond the memorial, north of the Flower Walk, there was once a mound known as the Mount. It was formed from

Coalbrookdale Gates

The Mount and revolving summerhouse, designed by William Kent in 1734 for George II and Queen Caroline. This drawing, dated 1736, is by Bernard Lens

earth excavated from the Serpentine and on it Queen Caroline had a summerhouse that revolved to catch the sun. This mound was eventually levelled. There are more fine trees here: a pyramidal hornbeam (*Carpinus betulus* 'Fastigiata'), a tree of heaven (*Ailanthus altissima*) near the memorial and a deciduous camellia (*Stuartia pseudocamellia*) at the end of the walk. The rarest tree in the park, however, is to be found at the south-east corner of the Albert Memorial. It is the Syrian maple (*Acer syriacum*), whose spreading branches form a mound-like canopy.

The final stop is the Serpentine Gallery, a handsome redbrick building put up as a refreshment room in 1934. It now displays Arts Council exhibitions of contemporary art. On the front lawn there are two beautiful golden Indian bean trees (*Catalpa bignonioides* 'Aurea'), whose leaves open bronze but become bright yellow in autumn.

In 1996–7 the Scottish poet and artist Ian Hamilton Finlay installed a permanent artwork at the Serpentine. It consists of a plaque on a tree at the end of the lawn, eight benches in the seating area, and a large round slate at the entrance dedicated to Diana, Princess of Wales. Each of these is inscribed with pastoral poetry, and the slate carries a quotation by the early 18th-century moral philosopher Francis Hutcheson: 'The beauty of trees, their cool shades, and their aptness to conceal from observation, have made groves and woods the usual retreat to those who love solitude, especially to the religious, the pensive, the melancholy, and the amorous.'

Hamilton Finlay's work at the Serpentine Gallery lies firmly within the English landscaping tradition that he so much admires. He has said that superior gardens are composed of glooms and solitudes, not plants and trees. They have a moral purpose, to elevate nature and add a spiritual dimension to human life.

Tree of heaven (*Ailanthus altissima*)

The Serpentine Gallery and golden Indian bean trees (*Catalpa bignonioides* 'Aurea')

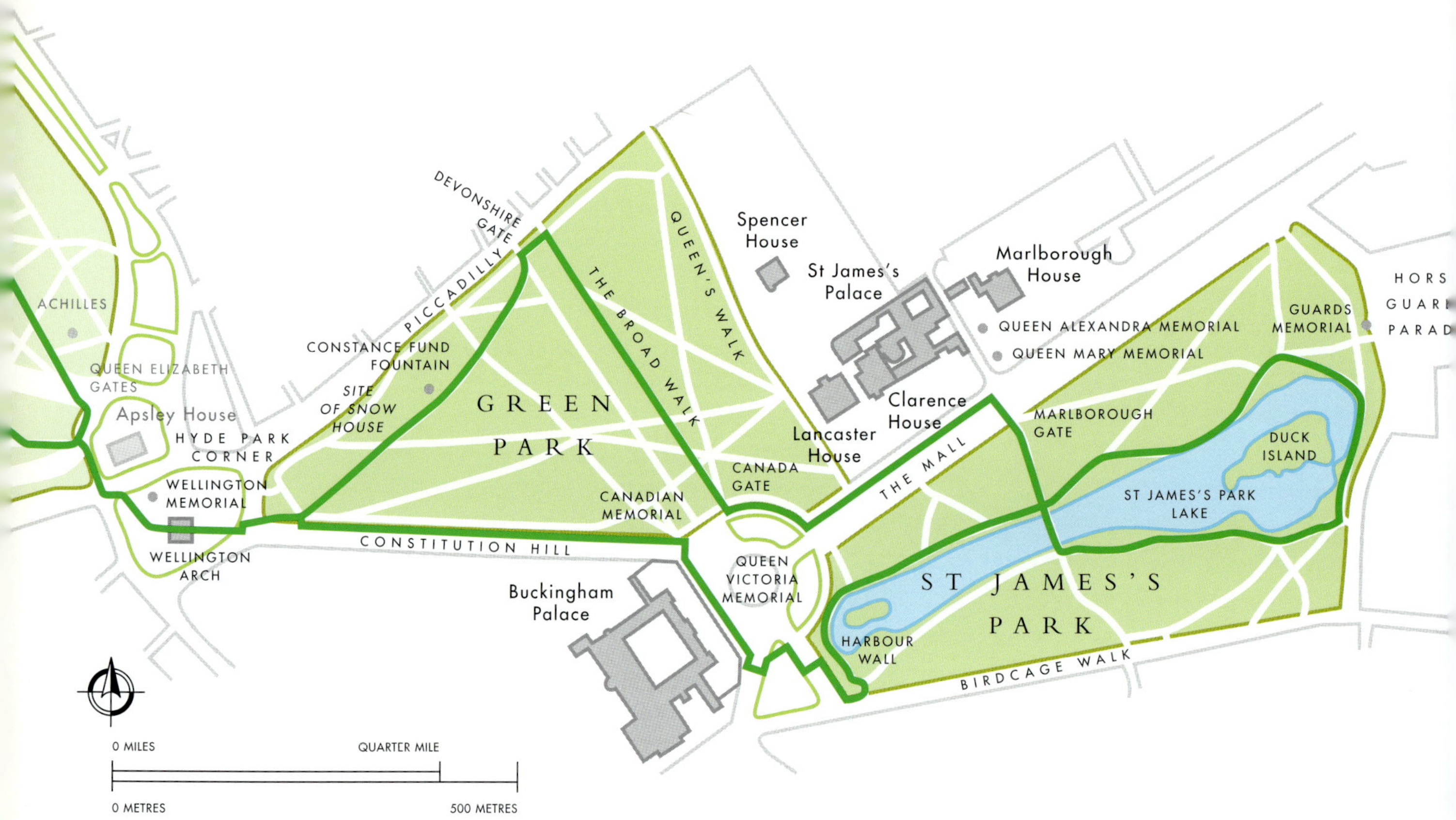
ACHILLES
QUEEN ELIZABETH GATES
Apsley House
HYDE PARK CORNER
WELLINGTON MEMORIAL
WELLINGTON ARCH
DEVONSHIRE GATE
PICCADILLY
CONSTANCE FUND FOUNTAIN
SITE OF SNOW HOUSE
GREEN PARK
THE BROAD WALK
QUEEN'S WALK
CANADIAN MEMORIAL
CONSTITUTION HILL
Spencer House
St James's Palace
Marlborough House
Clarence House
Lancaster House
CANADA GATE
THE MALL
Buckingham Palace
QUEEN VICTORIA MEMORIAL
QUEEN ALEXANDRA MEMORIAL
QUEEN MARY MEMORIAL
GUARDS MEMORIAL
HORS
GUAR
PARAD
MARLBOROUGH GATE
DUCK ISLAND
ST JAMES'S PARK LAKE
ST JAMES'S PARK
HARBOUR WALL
BIRDCAGE WALK
0 MILES
QUARTER MILE
0 METRES
500 METRES

Green Park and St James's Park

THE third part of the walk goes through Green Park and ends in St James's Park, which lies at the hub of royal life and ceremony. Crossing Hyde Park Corner, the route passes the memorial to the Duke of Wellington by J. E. Boehm (1888) with the Duke riding his favourite horse, Copenhagen. Wellington Arch (formerly Constitution Arch) in the centre was designed in 1828 by Decimus Burton as part of his new western approach to Buckingham Palace and was once surmounted by a colossal statue of Wellington. It is now crowned by a bronze group (1912) by Adrian Jones showing the figure of Peace descending from Heaven in the chariot of War, bringing the horses to a dramatic halt. The horses alone are so large that the sculptor, who had previously spent 24 years as an army vet, was able to hold a dinner party inside one of them to celebrate his achievement.

Green Park is an oasis of calm lying between the hustle and bustle of Piccadilly and the pomp of The Mall. Among its tall, stately trees it is pleasant to surrender to a 'green thought in a green shade' and recall that this rolling terrain was once wasteland. In Queen Elizabeth's time children used to come bird's-nesting here and John Gerard, the herbalist, found bugloss in the 'drie ditch banks about Pikadilla'.

The Queen's Basin, Green Park

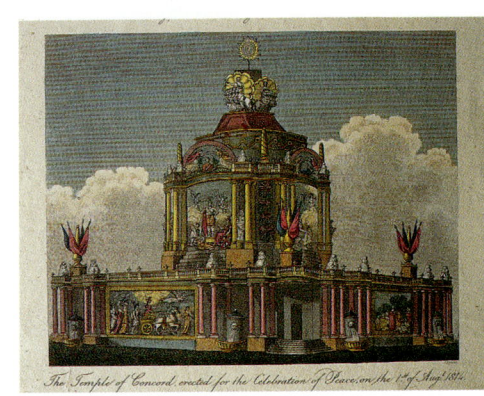

The Temple of Concord, 1814, Green Park

London plane (*Platanus* x *acerifolia*), Green Park

In 1688 the park was enclosed by Charles II, perhaps to prevent development in St James's from spreading westwards and cutting off Whitehall from Hyde Park. Stocked with deer and provided with a ranger's house, it was known as Upper St James's Park. By 1746 it was called Green Park and had become more of a pleasure garden. There was a reservoir in the north-east corner called the Queen's Basin, made to supply water to St James's Palace and Buckingham House, and beside it Queen's Walk, which had been planted by Queen Caroline and was a very fashionable venue. The Queen also commissioned William Kent to design her a library overlooking the park. Unfortunately this was damaged in 1749 when the huge Temple of Peace, erected to mark the end of the War of Austrian Succession, exploded during the opening firework display. Only Handel's Firework Music survived the occasion. Another explosion scarred the park in 1814 during the festivities for the Prince Regent's gala when its centrepiece, the Temple of Concord, also exploded. It had been designed by Sir William Congreve, the inventor of the military rocket.

In the course of time the few buildings that once dotted the park have been removed. All that remains of the Snow House put up for Charles II, 'as the mode is in some parts of France and Italy, and other hot countries, for to cool wines and other drinks for the summer season', is a mound to the left of the route. Just off its north-east corner is an enormous and very unusual plane tree, *Platanus* x *acerifolia* 'Augustine Henry'. The London plane is a hybrid descended from the oriental plane (*Platanus orientalis*) and the western plane (*Platanus occidentalis*). As with people, the individual specimens are not uniform but show a range of characteristics inherited from their various ancestors, and some are more resistant to pollution and fungus attack than others. 'Augustine Henry' is especially vigorous. Its leaves are a better green than those of other cultivars and nearly twice as big, up to 38cm (15in) wide. Most of the other trees in Green Park are plane or lime, with the occasional group of maples and flowering hawthorns. There is little wildlife of note in the park, though redwings and fieldfares are sometimes seen in the winter months.

Just beyond the site of the Snow House is the Constance Fund fountain (1954) by E. J. Clack, with Diana the naked huntress as elegant and swift as her hound. A little further on, on the left, are the Devonshire Gates, which were installed in 1921 in an attempt to create a formal axis along the Broad Walk to the new Canada Gate and the new Queen Victoria Memorial. They came from Devonshire House in Piccadilly but had been made in 1735 for Lord Heathfield's house at Turnham Green. Sphinxes rest on their splendid Palladian pillars.

The Constance Fund fountain

Devonshire Gates

The Broad Walk, Green Park

Canada Gate

Spencer House

The Broad Walk passes through the heart of Green Park to emerge at The Mall. On the left can be seen the handsome Palladian façade of Spencer House. At the end of the Broad Walk, on the right, is the Canadian Memorial (1994) by Pierre Granche, a strange abstract construction that is worth a brief inspection. Swinging left into The Mall, the route passes Lancaster House, faced, like Apsley House, in yellow Bath stone. It was intended for Frederick, Duke of York, who became heir to the throne after the death of the Prince Regent's daughter Princess Charlotte, but died in 1827 leaving the house unfinished. It is now used for government receptions and conferences. The architects Benjamin Dean Wyatt, Robert Smirke and, later, Charles Barry were responsible for the design. Beyond it is Clarence House, the home of the Queen Mother.

The Canadian Memorial

On the far corner, as the route turns into St James's, is Marlborough House, which was built in 1709–11 by Christopher Wren for Sarah, Duchess of Marlborough. She was a forthright woman and required a house that was 'strong, plain and convenient'. The red bricks were brought as ballast from the Netherlands in the ships that delivered troops and supplies to the Duke's armies. It the early 20th century it was the home of the widowed Queen Alexandra, who is commemorated by a memorial on the side wall, and of Queen Mary, whose plaque (1970) by William Reid Dick faces The Mall. The tribute to Queen

Marlborough House

Alexandra is by Sir Alfred Gilbert, to whom the Queen had shown great kindness. Its gothicised Art Nouveau style harks back to the 1890s, though the work was erected as late as 1932.

The Mall itself has been the scene of the most poignant, the most solemn, the most triumphant moments in the history of the British monarchy: countless state visits and royal weddings, the Golden Jubilee of Queen Victoria, the Silver Jubilee of Elizabeth II, and most recent of all, Princess Diana's funeral. On the morning of 6 September 1997 the cortège set off from the Queen's Chapel, was joined by the Prince of Wales and his sons at the junction with The Mall, and travelled slowly through Admiralty Arch to Westminster.

Yet, originally The Mall was conceived as a games pitch. Its creation dates to the 1660s, when Charles II decided to landscape St James's Park for the first time and to lay out an alley for the fashionable game of *paille-maille*, which until then had been played a short distance to the north. The park had been enclosed by Henry VIII when he built St James's Palace, and was used for hunting and exercise: there was a tiltyard and bowling alley here, and a cockpit at Whitehall. Charles, inspired by the splendid gardens he had seen during his exile, imposed a more formal scheme on the low-lying ground, with a long, straight canal lined with trees and a *patte d'oie,* or goosefoot, layout at the Whitehall end. André Le Nôtre, gardener to Louis XIV, has been associated with the design but it is more likely to be the work of the Mollet brothers, who were lodged in St James's Park in 1661. Despite these changes, the park retained a very rural character. A French visitor in 1694 described it as 'a large extent of ground set with walks and trees all round which were very agreeable. There is a canal in the middle edged with trees where one may see the ducks swimming; the rest is Meadow, and Pasture for the deer and cows. Its great Beauty consists in bringing (as it were) the Country into the City.'

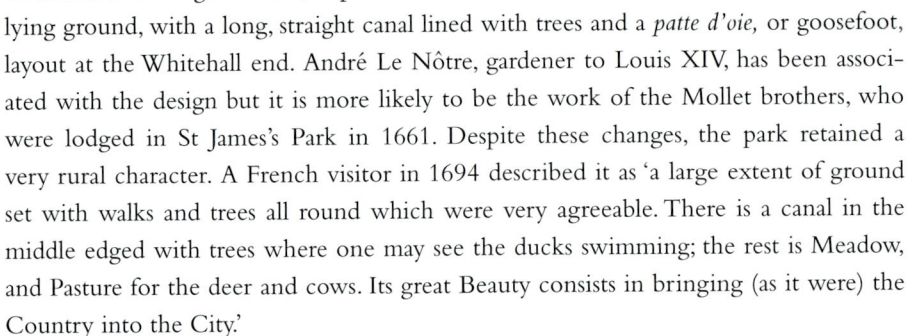

The King, determined to win the favour of his subjects, was on view here, strolling with his mistresses and dogs or playing *paille-maille* with 'matchless force' and 'graceful mien'. Pepys came regularly to St James's and reported in his diary that he had been 'discoursing with the keeper of the Pell Mell, who was sweeping of it, who told me of what the earth is mixed that do floor The Mall, and that over all there is cockle shells powdered and spread to keep it fast, which however in dry weather, turns to dust and deads the ball.'

In the 18th century the park became a busy and somewhat disreputable venue for Londoners of all classes. Although the gates were locked at night, there were a great many keyholders – official and unofficial – and the park became the haunt of whores, suicides and 'Mohawks', gangs of drunken young men who enjoyed taunting other visitors. Finally, when George III acquired Buckingham House in 1762 he decided to take matters in hand and appointed 'Capability' Brown as Royal Gardener. His landscaping proposal was never adopted, and it was left to John Nash to redesign the park in the 1820s, when he rebuilt Buckingham House for George IV.

Queen Alexandra Memorial

Queen Mary Memorial

The open lawn just inside Marlborough Gate makes a convenient place to pause and consider Nash's work. He replaced the old-fashioned canal with a lake, three islands and serpentine planting, and used the excavated earth to build up Carlton House Terrace, on the north side of park. The concept was similar to Capability Brown's proposal and has been preserved to this day, making the inner park one of the finest pieces of Picturesque landscaping in London. Since efforts have been made to respect Nash's concept, the planting of St James's is very different from that of other Royal Parks. Tall trees, many of them plane trees, provide the basic framework but the flowerbeds and many spreading and pendular trees, arranged informally, give it a more ornamental character.

The route crosses the park by the bridge built in 1957 by Eric Bedford in place of the original suspension bridge. This was the site of another devastating explosion at the Prince Regent's 1814 gala. The Chinese pagoda (one of Nash's first contributions to the Royal Parks) was illuminated, rather too generously, with gas lights, fireworks and rockets and it burst into flames, toppling into the canal before the eyes of the assembled dignitaries.

On one side of the bridge extends one of the most magnificent views in London, with Buckingham Palace, flanked by weeping willows, at one end and the towers of the Foreign Office breaking the skyline at the other. Behind the Foreign Office, is the great arc of the London Eye, a fairground halo revolving almost imperceptibly over the city. It was installed for the Millennium and, to the relief of some and the regret of others, is meant to be temporary.

St James's Park lake

The Pagoda Bridge, St James's Park, 1814

View to Whitehall, St James's Park lake

Weeping beech (*Fagus sylvatica* 'Pendula')

On the other side of the lake the path leads past many interesting trees. There is a large weeping beech (*Fagus sylvatica* 'Pendula') on the corner, and on the mound to the right some mulberry trees (*Morus nigra*) planted as a reminder of the unsuccessful silk industry founded by James I. On the lake shore there are weeping hazels (*Corylus avellana* 'Pendula') and a group of enormous, spreading fig trees (*Ficus carica*).

Duck Island was formed when Nash made the lake, and on it there is a *cottage orné* built in 1840 by J. B. Watson for the Ornithological Society. Wildfowl have always been an important feature of the park, enjoyed by all and sundry; hard-pressed government ministers have even been known to rehearse their speeches before an appreciative audience of pelicans. A Keeper of Ponds was first recorded in 1572 and later decoys, a pool and a hide were added. James I installed aviaries in nearby Birdcage Walk, and Storey's Gate takes its name from Edward Storey, Keeper of the King's Birds. John Evelyn, in the 1670s, found 'numerous flocks of severall sorts of ordinary and extraordinary wilde fowle, breeding about the Decoy, which for being neere so great a city and among such a concourse of soldiers and people, is a singular and diverting thing. … There were withy-potts or nests for the wild fowle to lay their eggs in, a little above ye surface of ye water.'

Duck Island Cottage

The first pelicans were the gift of the Russian ambassador in 1664. They are spectacular birds with the disconcerting habit of swallowing live fish under the eyes of visitors. Despite this, they are peaceful creatures. Both mute and black swans nest in the park, as do tufted duck, pochard, shovelers, pintails, coots, moorhen and mallard. Other nesting species include the tawny owl, blue tit, great tit, grey wagtail and jay. Many of the birds are migratory, and pass through in spring and autumn, or winter in the park after spending the summer months in Finland or Russia. The visitors include: pied flycatchers, wheatears, warblers, swallows and martins, tufted ducks, wigeon, teal and shoveler. The smew, goldeneye and merganser are captive species. Chivvying the other birds and fighting for food are the black-headed gulls that arrive from July onwards, while soaring above the busy scene is often a sparrowhawk or kestrel. On the north side of the lake there are useful information boards on this birdlife.

Horse Guards Parade

The Foreign Office, where the kestrels are thought to nest, presides over the eastern end of the park. It forms part of the Government Offices (1868–73) designed by George Gilbert Scott. Their Italianate style was the outcome of a lengthy battle with Lord Palmerston, the Prime Minister, who rejected the architect's initial proposal for Gothic and also his attempt at an Italo-Byzantine scheme. Eventually, Scott 'bought some costly books on Italian architecture' and came up with an acceptable solution. On the left-hand corner is a statue of Lord Mountbatten by the Czech sculptor Franta Belsky (1983). It shows Mountbatten in his favourite post as First Sea Lord, surveying Horse Guards Parade whose ceremonies he so enjoyed. This was once the site of Henry VIII's tiltyard but has been a parade ground since the late 17th century. The Trooping the Colour ceremony, celebrating the Queen's official birthday, is held here in June. The Horse Guards building, a peculiarly staccato and agitated example of English Palladianism, was designed by William Kent but executed after his death in 1748 by John Vardy.

Circling the lake, the path goes past a fine medlar tree (*Mespilus germanica*) and then swings left just before the Guards Memorial (1922), which is by H. Carlton Bradshaw, with sculpture by Gilbert Ledward. The five soldiers aligned in front represent the Grenadier, Coldstream, Scots, Irish and Welsh Guards. The panel on the rear shows a field gun in action. Ledward's work, though naturally conservative, was very fine and he was one of the few leading artists to devote himself entirely to war memorials.

Guards Memorial

A classic view from the St James's Park lake

A little further on is a young ginkgo or maidenhair tree (*Ginkgo biloba*). This species is the only living representative of the botanical order known as Ginkgoales, which is known from fossils to have lived around 250 million years ago but is otherwise extinct. Planted since ancient times in Chinese and Japanese temple gardens, there is much debate as to whether it survives in the wild. The massive column that can be seen behind the shrubbery is the memorial to the Duke of York by Richard Westmacott (1834). The expenditure on Lancaster House left him heavily in debt, and it was said he was placed on a column to escape the claims of his creditors.

A milk fair was established in the park in 1666 and a French visitor wrote in the 18th century that cows were tethered and milked on the spot, the milk served 'with all the cleanliness peculiar to the English, in little mugs at the rate of 1d per mug'. The last stalls were removed in 1905.

Maidenhair tree (*Gingko biloba*)

At the western end of the lake is another island and beyond it the Harbour Wall, which was constructed in 1904 when the lake was shortened to make way for the Queen Victoria Memorial. Later the lake was cut back still further and a path made alongside the wall. Until 1770 there was a pool at this end of the park known as Rosamond's Lake. It was favoured by courting couples, but also won the epithet of Suicide Pond, and eventually was filled in. The are a number of interesting trees here: a swamp cypress (*Taxodium distichum*) on the left before the island, two pencil-thin Dawyck beeches (*Fagus sylvatica* 'Dawyck') on the lawn to the

The Milk Fair in Victorian times

Life Guards in The Mall

Victory surmounts the Queen Victoria Memorial

right, and a very fine copper beech (*Fagus sylvatica* 'Purpurea') around the head of the lake.

From here the route emerges from the park and eventually reaches the Queen Victoria Memorial in front of Buckingham Palace. In 1911 a processional route, devised by Sir Aston Webb, was laid out from Admiralty Arch to this grand *rond-point* in front of Buckingham Palace. The Memorial was its climax. The Queen (an undistinguished work by Thomas Brock) is flanked by the figures of Truth, Justice and Charity and surmounted by a heavily gilded Victory. Around the podium (which symbolises British sea power) are bronze groups representing Progress, Peace, Manufacture and Agriculture, each accompanied by a lion. Painting and Architecture, Shipbuilding and Mining face each other above the basin on the east and west sides of the memorial. Unfortunately, by the time the memorial was completed in 1911 its rhetoric was outmoded, but although it is now out of fashion – and likely to remain so – it remains an appropriate symbol of the empire on which it seemed the sun would never set.

Finally, the route returns to Hyde Park Corner, past the high wall that screens Buckingham Palace gardens with its lake and flamingos and up Constitution Hill, so named because Charles II took his exercise (or 'constitutional') here. The road has a surprisingly eventful history: on three separate occasions Queen Victoria was attacked by lunatics on Constitution Hill and in 1850 Sir Robert Peel suffered fatal injuries when he was thrown from his horse at the upper end.

Celebrating the 50th anniversary of VJ Day, 1995

The Queen Victoria Memorial

Select Bibliography

HRH The Princess of Wales, The Public Life by Tom Corby
The Royal Family and the Spencers by Nerina Shute
Georgiana, Duchess of Devonshire by Amanda Foreman
Diana, Princess of Wales, A Tribute by Tim Graham and Tom Corby
Inside Kensington Palace by Andrew Morton
The Buildings of England: London, 1, The Cities of London and Westminster by N. Pevsner and B. Cherry
Wildlife in the Royal Parks by E. Simms
The Royal Parks of London by G. Williams
The London Encyclopaedia eds. B. Weinreb and C. Hibbert
Trees of the Royal Parks by J. G. Berry
Buildings and Monuments in the Royal Parks by Lucy Trench

For further information on the trees, plants and wildlife in the parks, contact the London Natural History Society (c/o The Natural History Museum, Cromwell Road, London SW7 5BD) and the London Wildlife Trust (80 York Way, London N1 9AG). Both publish newsletters and journals.

Some Royal Parks publications

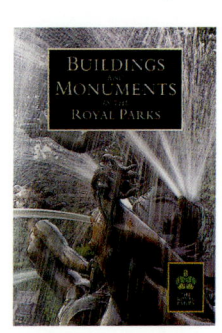

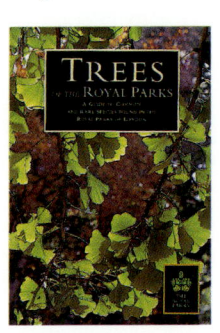

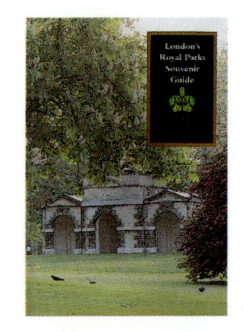